Painting the Sky

writing POETRY with children

Painting the Sky

writing POETRY with children

Shelley Tucker, M. Ed.

Illustrated by Margaret Anne Suggs

GoodYearBooks

An Imprint of ScottForesman
A Division of HarperCollinsPublishers

GoodYearBooks are available for
most basic curriculum subjects plus
many enrichment areas. For more
GoodYearBooks, contact your local
bookseller or educational dealer. For a
complete catalog with information about
other GoodYearBooks, please write:

GoodYearBooks
ScottForesman
1900 East Lake Avenue
Glenview, IL 60025

This book is for Caitlin Wilson, age 4,
who speaks and lives poetry.

"The hearts are writing poetry."

Caitlin Wilson

"He...who aspires to be a great poet,
must first become a little child."

Thomas Babington Macaulay

Thanks

Thank you to all the teachers and
students who write and value poetry. My deep appreciation to the
following people: Lauren Wilson for continuing to share poetry
ideas; Barry Calhoun for developing the castle book; my husband,
Bruce Sherman, Chickie Kitchman, Sue Berlin, and Lynn Keat for
their constant love and support; Nora Mahoney for assistance on
my last book; and all of the participants in my "Write from the
Source, Poetry Writing Workshops" who show the honesty,
celebration, and community available through writing poetry. My
appreciation to the following writers for the many ways their
works have contributed to my thoughts on poetry and writing:
Christina Baldwin, George Lakoff, Mark Johnson, Donald Graves,
Natalie Goldberg, and Barbara Kingsolver.

CONTENTS

1   # POETRY WRITING IS A BRIDGE

1   Concepts vs. Structures,
or Why It is Easier for Most People to Write Personification Than Haiku

2   Poetic Concepts and Writing Success

3   Poetry Writing and Skill Development

4   Spelling, Editing, and Punctuation

5   The Importance of Reading Poetry Aloud

6   Guidelines for Reading and Listening

7   Discussions About Poetry

8   # HOW TO USE THIS BOOK

8   Poetry Units

9   Other Classroom Uses for the Worksheets

9   Poetry Assignments in School and the Evaluation of Poetry

10   Poetry Writing and Parts of Speech

11   Figurative and Literal Language

12   Poetry Writing and Other Language Arts Skills

12   Making Lists

13   Poetry Writing, Science, Social Studies, and Other Subjects

14   Poetry Writing and Factual Information in Subject Areas

15   # MAKING BOOKS

From *Painting the Sky: Writing Poetry with Children* published by GoodYearBooks. Copyright © 1995 Shelley Tucker.

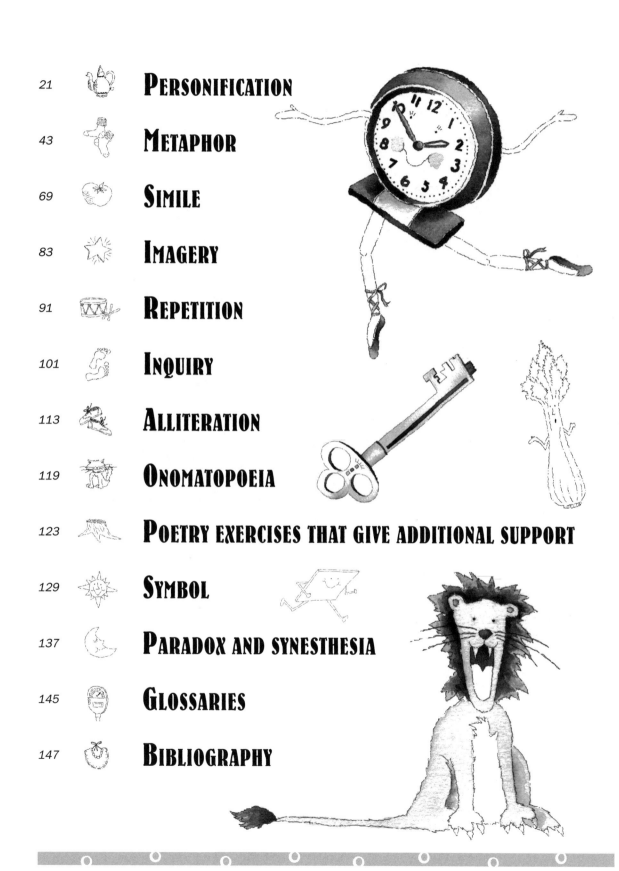

21 PERSONIFICATION

43 METAPHOR

69 SIMILE

83 IMAGERY

91 REPETITION

101 INQUIRY

113 ALLITERATION

119 ONOMATOPOEIA

123 POETRY EXERCISES THAT GIVE ADDITIONAL SUPPORT

129 SYMBOL

137 PARADOX AND SYNESTHESIA

145 GLOSSARIES

147 BIBLIOGRAPHY

POETRY WRITING IS A BRIDGE

Poetry writing is a bridge that connects children to the relevance of writing, reading, learning, honesty, and community. Passage on this bridge is open to all children, and successful crossings are guaranteed. This is because poetry writing relies on the senses, emotions, and history of each child. Success as a poetry writer is not dependent on academic achievement. Rather, poetry writing and sharing pave the way for greater social development and academic success.

Concepts vs. Structures, or Why It Is Easier for Most People to Write Personification Than Haiku

Poetry writing is usually taught to children through the use of structures, like limericks, haiku, and cinquains. This structured approach often stresses rhyme patterns, word counts, and syllabication rather than content.

There are a number of limitations in the use of set structures to teach poetry writing. Children often feel locked into forms which neither adhere to standard English language nor provide enough space for them to express their thoughts. As a result, they change their ideas to fit the forms, losing the immediacy and accuracy of their original thoughts and feelings. Because children often see poetry structures as external to the ways they think and speak, they usually stop writing poems after a unit of poetry instruction.

Teach children to write with poetic elements, like metaphors, similes, and personification, and they learn ways to easily express their thoughts and emotions. Rather than limit ideas, feelings, and memories to fit forms, poetic elements are the concepts that carry and expand thought. Children find poetic elements easy to understand and apply because these forms are present in everyday language. When children write with poetic elements, they learn relevant, lifelong ways to conceptualize and express their thoughts and feelings.

Poetic Concepts and Writing Success

The following describe some of the achievements by children who wrote and shared poetry based on poetic concepts. These are successes of:

- The child who carried her book of poems with her throughout the day. Her poetry provided clear and tangible proof of her accomplishment.
- The children who arrived at school early and stayed late to write poems.
- The class of children who learned a wide array of math skills as they discussed how to price and sell their books.
- The fourth-grade boy from a violent family who wrote and published volumes of poetry. He received considerable attention for his books and had his first school year without being expelled.
- The girl who became confident when she visited elementary classrooms and read her poems to younger children.
- The boy whose poetry inspired him to write novels and plays.
- The children who at first intimidated younger students but then decided to form poetry writing clubs for them instead.
- The excitement and pride that were evident when all children in a class succeeded at the same poetry writing assignments.
- The students with special needs who gained conceptual thinking skills and confidence in their

ability to learn. These same children moved out of special classes to become teachers, firefighters, mechanics, writers, etc.—contributing citizens with respect and appreciation for the power of language.

- The schools where the breakdown of cliques and the formation of classroom communities occurred because children openly and honestly shared their histories and feelings through poetry writing and reading.
- The children who saw, through poetry writing, that their words mattered.

Poetry Writing and Skill Development

Children who write, share, and publish poems learn and succeed in many ways. Poetry writing encourages them to:

- Excel at a form of creative expression—everyone can compose good poetry
- Expand oral and written vocabulary
- Generalize poetic skills to other forms of writing
- Broaden the ways they see the world by showing them connections between people, places, and things
- Accept tangible proof of their accomplishment
- Frame their thoughts and feelings. Record the present and explore the past
- Develop deep connections to their feelings and senses
- Form groups where children openly share and attentively listen
- Increase their confidence when they read and present to groups
- Experience the joy that comes from noticing, through poetry writing, daily events like the sound of a bird or the color of the sky
- Expand their thinking skills

Spelling, Editing, and Punctuation

Accurate spelling is a mechanical skill while poetry writing is a creative one. When children receive spellings from adults or dictionaries during the rough or first draft phase of their writing, they interrupt the spontaneous and creative flow of their ideas. Encourage students to use "inventive," "made-up," "guess and go," or "rough draft" spellings when they first write their poems. They then correct any misspelled words during the rewrite phase.

Many people think of editing as a hammer that bangs their poems into splinters. Editing poetry, however, can be a gentle process, like watching a bird as it slows down and comes clearly into view. Suggest that children read their poems to themselves and others to notice, delete, and change words and ideas to create more exact sounds, meanings, and rhythms.

The layout of a poem contributes to its meaning. Many children initially write their poems in paragraph form. To punctuate poetry, ask children to reread their writing and draw a diagonal line (/) every place they pause. When they rewrite their poems, each mark indicates where they begin a new line.

Punctuation of poetry and prose can be complementary rather than competitive. Ask students to place a capital letter at the start of each sentence and a question mark or period at the end. A poem written in this way is also easier to read and understand:

> In the springtime,
> rain beats down on my window
> with the quick drumming sounds
> of bongos in the night.

The Importance of Reading Poetry Aloud

WORDS

When someone else hears my words,
I feel the addition of the second voice
added to my own.
My words, theirs,
the idea grows.
And when the third
is added to the first two
and the fourth
to the three,
my voice is no longer alone.
It is a trumpet.

Andrea Brice, adult

The interplay between writing poetry and reading it out loud is critical for a number of reasons:

1. Sound is part of the meaning of a poem. When children read their poems orally, they hear the sound of their words and its influence on the meaning of their writing.
2. People listen carefully to poems that reflect the real feelings and thoughts of the writers. The praise is spontaneous and genuine.
3. Poems read silently focus on the visual process. When children read poetry aloud, the sound is emphasized, and they hear where they need to edit their work.
4. Reading out loud is an integral part of poetry. Poems, then, have multiple modalities.
5. One of the goals of adults is to prepare children to be thoughtful and active citizens. When children read their poems aloud and are heard, they receive tangible proof that their ideas, creativity, feelings, and words matter.

Guidelines for Reading and Listening

Establish guidelines so children feel safe when they read their poetry out loud. The following are the types of guidelines educators and group leaders might present to children:

1. If you talk about your poetry before or after you read it aloud, you may:

   a. Make positive statements about it.

   b. Comment on the progress of your poem.

   It is fine to say: "I'm still working on this," or "This is in progress." *(Do not criticize your writing.)*

2. When someone else reads poetry out loud, you may:

   a. Listen.

   b. Continue to write.

   c. Draw a picture related to your poem.

   (Do not talk or make noises when someone is reading aloud.)

3. You have a number of choices in how you respond to another person's poetry.

   a. Praise the poem. There are many ways to express praise:

      1. Comment on a word, line, or stanza.

      2. Listen quietly. Silence is often a sign of respect.

      3. Clap.

      4. Wave your hands in the air, place your hands on your heart, or make some other positive motions with your hands.

      5. Praise the structure of the poem. *(e.g. "I like the repetition.")*

      6. Ask the writer to reread the poem out loud.

   b. Say how you feel when you hear the poem.

   c. Ask a question.

   d. Ask if the reader if he or she wants to hear you comments.

   (Do not criticize anyone else's writing.)

From *Painting the Sky: Writing Poetry with Children* published by GoodYearBooks. Copyright ©1995 Shelley Tucker.

Discussions About Poetry

At Home

Ask children some or all of the following:

Where/How did you get the idea for your poem?

What do you see or feel when you read it?

What parts of your poem do you particularly like?

Would you like to publish this poem?

At School

Please consider these guidelines:

1. Ask students the types of questions listed above.
2. Conference with them about measurable behaviors. *(Please refer to the next section.)* **Students see grading standards as fair when they understand criteria for the evaluation.**

HOW TO USE THIS BOOK

Poetry Units

Eleven poetry writing units are presented in this book. Each unit consists of an introduction to the concept, a handout of writing exercises, and a page of sample poems illustrating that concept. Poetry writing can be a life-long mode of expression, and the inclusion in this book of poems by both children and adults shows that people of all ages can succeed in the same creative process. The authors of the poems come from a wide variety of settings. Their ages are listed next to their names.

The exercises in this book develop the elements of poetry already present in everyday language and thought. Children naturally use metaphor, alliteration, and other poetic language when they talk, and with instruction can easily transfer these concepts to their writing.

Each worksheet can be used as a separate writing activity, a part of a larger unit on a specific poetic element *(such as metaphor)*, or a component in a writing program that teaches figurative language throughout the year. Please feel free to modify these exercises or develop new ones from ideas presented in the chapter introductions. Writing poetry is like planting and growing a garden. The goal of these exercises and ideas is to cultivate the rich field of student imagination and productivity.

It is important, therefore, to allow children to choose their topics. This ensures that their writing will be interesting and relevant to them. At school, apply class rules that govern appropriate language and topics to the poetry writing assignments.

From *Painting the Sky: Writing Poetry with Children* published by GoodYearBooks. Copyright ©1995 Shelley Tucker.

Other Classroom Uses for the Worksheets

Use this book at home, in clubs, or at school. Poetry writing activities, assignments, and skills provide natural complements to other subject areas:

> Combine poetry writing with the instruction of parts of speech *(see page 10)*.
>
> Reinforce other language arts skills, such as the development of figurative and literal thought, through poetry writing *(see page 12)*.
>
> Use poetry writing and reading to complement social studies, science, and other subject areas, such as foreign languages *(see page 13)*.

Poetry Assignments in School and the Evaluation of Poetry

The following are examples of poetry writing assignments for the instruction of metaphors:

> Assign one or two of these at a time:
>
> Write at least 20 metaphors.
>
> Expand at least 10 of these metaphors by answering: Who? What? Where? Why? or How?
>
> Write two poems. Each poem must have at least eight lines. Include at least one metaphor per poem.
>
> Say or write, from memory, the definition of a metaphor.
>
> Rewrite one poem, in poetic form, with correct spellings.
>
> Explain your use of punctuation, line breaks, and capitals you use in your final draft.
>
> Read at least one of your poems to the class.

A critique is one person's opinion or perception about the quality of a poem. Unfortunately, a critique is often offered as fact rather than opinion. Students feel encouraged when they are evaluated on completion of measurable assignments rather than rated on the perceived quality of their poems. Written evaluations can include combinations of pluses, checks, and minuses to show which of the criteria have been met. Students stay motivated when they are permitted to redo assignments to meet all of the goals.

Because each poem is a success, avoid the use of number or letter grades on poetry. Letters and numbers tell children that poems are ladders that can be climbed up to As or tumbled down to Fs. Children do not write good or bad poems. Rather, they compose poetry people like or dislike, or they write poems that do or don't address the assignments. Poems are like stars. Each one helps light up the night sky.

Poetry Writing and Parts of Speech

Natural pairings occur between the poetic elements taught in this workbook and the parts of speech *(such as nouns or prepositions)* used to write them. Consider teaching elements of poetry and parts of speech in the following pairs:

Poetic Element	Part of Speech	Worksheet Title	Page
personification	personal pronouns	Honest Potatoes	*23*
		Trucks Giggle	*27*
		Blue Dreams	*33*
		Tomato Daze	*37*
	action verbs	Listen to the Sea	*25*
		Trucks Giggle	*27*
		Blue Dreams	*33*
		Buses Wheeze	*39*
		All worksheets	*48-67*
metaphors	nouns	All worksheets	*68-79*
similes	nouns	Laughter Is As Old	*74*
	adjectives	Fast As Popcorn	*78*

From *Painting the Sky: Writing Poetry with Children* published by GoodYearBooks. Copyright ©1995 Shelley Tucker.

Poetic Element	Part of Speech	Worksheet Title	Page
imagery	action verbs	Red Slides	*86*
		Action	*88*
repetition	subordinating conjunctions	Introduction	*91*
inquiry	adverbs	Introduction	*91*
	prepositions	Behind Night	*92, 93*
		Inside	*95*
inquiry	adverbs *(e.g. who, what)*	What's in the Ocean?	*104*
		Invention	*102*
		What does this key unlock?	*105*
		What If Time	*107*
		What's Inside the Alphabet	*109*
		What If We Exchanged	*111*
alliteration	adjectives	Bashful Banana	*116*
onomatopoeia	action verbs	Purple Roars	*125*
symbol	nouns	Eyes	*131, 132*
		Gold	*134, 135*

Figurative and Literal Language

The following poetry models use both figurative and literal language, and allow poets to understand the difference between them:

Worksheet Name	Page
White is Time Ticking	*55*
What's in the Ocean?	*100*
What does this key unlock?	*104*

Poetry Writing and Other Language Arts Skills

Memorize the 5 Ws and H:

Who? What? Where? When? Why? How?

Use any of the 5 Ws or H to expand a basic metaphor, simile, or personification.

Example: Love is the sky *(How?)* open and *(Where?)* always around you.

Worksheet Name	Page
White is Time Ticking	*58*
What's in the Ocean?	*104*
Gold	*134, 135*

Making Lists

List making exercises children's ability to think. The following poetry models ask children to make and use lists:

Worksheet Name	Poetic Element	Page
Tomato Daze	personification	*37*
Extended Metaphor Explanation	metaphor	*44, 45*
Avocado Sky	metaphor	*64, 65*
Panther Moon		*61, 62*
Cinnamon Rain	metaphor	*67*
Basketball Is Like	simile	*70*
Red Slides into First Base	imagery	*86*
Action	imagery with verbs	*88*

From *Painting the Sky: Writing Poetry with Children* published by GoodYearBooks. Copyright © 1995 Shelley Tucker.

Worksheet Name	Poetic Element	Page
What's in the Ocean?	inquiry	*104*
Jelly Jams in Jars	alliteration	*114*
Yikes!	onomatopoeia	*120*
Eyes	symbol	*131, 132*
Gold	symbol	*134, 135*

Poetry Writing with Science, Social Studies, and Other Subject Areas

Poetry writing and sharing complement content areas. Nearly any subject in science and social studies works well with poetry writing. Math provides an array of topics, such as angles, polyhedrons, and measurements for use in poems. Home and family living offers definitions and recipes. Students use terms and topics from subject areas on the following worksheets:

Worksheet	Page
Trucks Giggle	*27*
Tomato Daze	*37*
All metaphor models	*48-67*
What's in the Ocean?	*104*
Invention	*102*
Jelly Jams in Jars	*114*

Poetry Writing and Factual Information in Subject Areas

Students accumulate facts about a specific subject, such as the solar system, and then use their information on the following worksheets:

Worksheet	Page
Honest Potatoes	23
Listen to the Sea	25
Circles Travel in Lines	41
I Am the Sea	49
Panther Moon	61, 62
Basketball Is Like	70
What's in the Ocean?	104

From *Painting the Sky: Writing Poetry with Children* published by GoodYearBooks. Copyright © 1995 Shelley Tucker.

MAKING BOOKS

"To have great poets, there must be great audiences, too."

Walt Whitman

Publishing plays a key role in the cycle of poetry that includes writing, reading, and listening. Books composed by children show them that their words are important, and provide them with clear demonstration of their accomplishments.

Poetry books reinforce both the process and product of writing. When children see their books displayed next to those of professional authors, they gain confidence in their ability to write. Books written and illustrated by children earn them sincere, spontaneous praise.

Children and adults can make the same types of books they see in stores. Some of these books take time to assemble, but book construction is like mining gems. The products are precious, and, like jewels, they last a lifetime.

Types of Books for Children and Adults to Make

Side Stapled Staple these books along the left sides or tops. They are easy and inexpensive to prepare.

Sewn Binding Punch three holes along the side of the book, and connect the holes with a piece of string or yarn. A textured or hand-drawn cover gives these books an antique appearance.

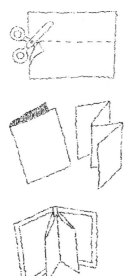

Accordion Books Cut a sheet of paper, 8 1/2 by 14 inches, in half, so the new dimensions are 4 1/4 by 14 inches. Hold the paper horizontally, and fold it in half. Then fold it in quarters by bringing the two ends out and up to meet the center crease. The result is a fold every 3 1/2 inches.

Cut two pieces of cardboard to measure 3 1/2 by 4 1/2 inches each. The cardboard becomes the front and back covers of the book. Cover each piece of cardboard with wallpaper, maps, construction paper, photographs, or rice paper. Tape or glue a two foot piece of ribbon or string on the unfinished side of each piece of cardboard.

Take the strip of paper and point the center crease up. Write poems or draw pictures on each of the four areas separated by folds. Glue each end of the strip of paper onto the unfinished side of a piece of cardboard. Fasten the book with the ribbon. Glue seashells, rocks, glitter, or dried flowers onto the cover.

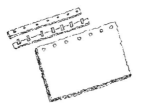

Velo-binding Personal Velo-binders are the size of three hole punches, and can be purchased at office supply stores. These machines punch a line of small holes on the side or top of the pages. A plastic strip, called a velo-binding, fits through the holes and fastens the book. Because the holes are so small, the process requires considerable manual dexterity. Velo-bindings are also available at copy stores.

From *Painting the Sky: Writing Poetry with Children* published by GoodYearBooks. Copyright ©1995 Shelley Tucker.

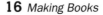

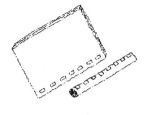

Comb Binding Comb binding machines are economical and available in most schools. These machines punch large holes into books which are then fastened with comb *(plastic)* binders. The opportunity to independently bind their books and the sound of the crunch of the paper provide extra interest to children. There are a variety of books that use comb bindings. Instruct children to follow these directions:

a. Standard Comb Bound Books:
Bind books across the sides or tops. Comb bindings are easy to cut, so these books can take a variety of dimensions. Art work, laminated collages, photographs, and copies of maps make interesting book covers.

b. Shape Books:
Create books in which all of the pages are in the shape of a flower, car, planet, or other object. Bind these books along a straight edge at the top or side of the shape. Make covers from tagboard, cover stock, or thin cardboard to give support for inside pages.

c. Shape Books with Center Bindings:
Books with symmetrical shapes provide extra interest when cut and then bound down the middle.

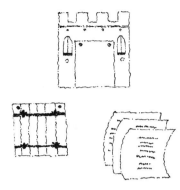

d. Castle Books:

A castle book reinforces the study of medieval times. This book uses a comb binding at the bottom. A drawbridge opens, and the poems are behind it.

On a piece of art paper, tagboard, or construction paper, draw a castle with a drawbridge in the middle. The drawbridge must come down to the bottom of the page. On a different sheet of paper, draw another drawbridge the same size as the original. This second drawbridge will move when the book is finished. Cut out the second drawbridge, and place it on top of the first. Punch two holes through both drawbridges, one set of holes at the top of the right side and the other set at the top of the left.

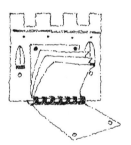

Then cut out paper for the poems. Use the dimensions of the drawbridge less one half an inch on the two long sides and top. Write poetry on this paper. Then insert these pages between the two drawbridges, lining up the bottoms of the paper and the drawbridges. Bind the book along the bottom of the drawbridges.

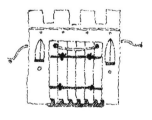

Take a long piece of yarn or string. Start behind the picture of the castle. Put one end of the yarn through the right holes in both drawbridges, across the front of the movable drawbridge, and through the left holes. Lower the drawbridge until it forms a right angle or "L." Tie the ends of the strings behind the castle. Use the yarn to open and shut the drawbridge.

From *Painting the Sky: Writing Poetry with Children* published by GoodYearBooks. Copyright ©1995 Shelley Tucker.

Center Stapled First, construct a model of the final book. Count all the pages *(e.g. title page, table of contents, credit page, number of poetry pages)* that will be in the book. This number must be divisible by four. If the total page count is 78, for example, two pages must be added or removed.

Use 80 total pages as the example. Divide 80 by four. The answer, 20, tells how many sheets of 8 1/2 x 11 paper, copied on both sides, are needed to construct an 80 page book. Each piece of paper in this type of book contains four poems *(or other components, like credit or title pages).* Two poems appear on the front of each sheet and two on the back. When folded down the center, the final book is approximately 5 1/2 x 8 1/2 inches in size.

To construct the model, turn the 20 sheets of paper, so the 8 1/2 inch dimension becomes the height. Fold the papers in half, so the left edges meet the right. Start on the first page, and write the name of what will appear there. Turn to the back of the front page. Will it be blank? If so, write, "Blank." If not, label what will appear on that page. Continue this process and fill in the entire model.

Now, get 20 new sheets of paper. Follow the order of the model, and type, paste, or use a computer to print or arrange the poems and other content. Copy the front of one sheet of paper onto the back of the next one, and fold the pages in half.

Next, prepare the covers. Cover paper should be sturdy to provide support for the book, yet thin enough to fold neatly. Tagboard and cover stock work well. Use cover paper that wraps around the book with at least one half inch extra on each side. This additional width and length make the cover easier to trim.

Staple the books in the center along the vertical fold. Have a copy store trim the right, top, and bottom edges.

Perfect Binding Perfect bindings are the standard glued bindings found on most of books sold in stores. They are done by binderies, and many companies are willing to take orders for a small number of books.

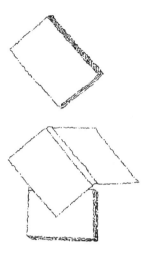

Construct books with perfect bindings the same way as those with center staples. There are, however, a few major differences. Do not fold the final copies. Instead, take the covers and double sided pages to the bindery. The binder then cuts the contents down the center, puts the two halves of the book together, glues the left side of the book to the cover, and trims the remaining edges.

Take time during all the phases of bookmaking. For many students, the proof of their writing success is the book. Carefully discuss, design, and prepare covers. Talk about titles. Choose bindings. Decide when and how books will be displayed. Plan poetry readings that include families and friends. Make extra books to give away as presents.

Look at books, show them to others, and reread them. Books circle children back through their lives, root them in the present, and, like the sun, light up the roads to the future.

From *Painting the Sky: Writing Poetry with Children* published by GoodYearBooks. Copyright ©1995 Shelley Tucker.

PERSONIFICATION

Personification is the assignment of human characteristics to things.

DINNER

Knife was the first to speak.
He was known mostly for his sharp cutting remarks.

Chairs sat down underneath the table.
Napkins folded themselves into their laps.

Teapot, unable to stand the tension, began to boil.

Cup held one hand on her hip
Knowing she could hold her own.

Fork and spoon huddled off to the side next to plate.
They knew plate could handle whatever was dished out.

Terry Garrison, adult

Until the middle of this century, most poems written in English rhymed at the ends of lines. Now free verse, poetry without end rhyme, meter, or set structure, offers more accessible options for poetry writing. Each chapter in this book presents one or two of the components of free verse.

Try this personification exercise. First name some things, like sky, trash, and chocolate. Next list actions *(verbs)* a person does. Then use some of the action words to describe the things. Consider the following examples:

Sky sings.
Trash sneezes.
Chocolate calls.

Now make the sentences longer by answering: Who?
What? Where? When? Why? or How?

Sky sings *(How?)* in harmony with the moon.

Trash sneezes *(Why?)* because I leave it on the porch for
   two weeks.

Chocolate calls *(Who?)* me, but I try not to listen.

Personification is easily transferred from thoughts and speech to writing. Poets make things seem like people in a variety of ways. To create personification, name an object, color, idea, or emotion. Then use some of the following to describe it.

Examples: human actions
               cars *laugh,* hope *winks*
            humans descriptions
               lazy vacuum cleaner, *smiling* moon
            human body parts
               tree's *legs,* truck's *eyes*
            human jobs, friends, foods hobbies, feelings
               Hope *works* in the bank. Her *friends*
               are courage and trust.
            personal pronouns
               She, he, his, her, they, or *them* instead
               of *it* when referring to the object

BRAVERY

Bravery lives in everyone.
Her favorite cousin is laughter.
Bravery vacations at Scarlet and Velvet's Hotel
on the Indigo Beach.
Bravery dreams about criticism
and how to prevent it.
Her favorite foods are chocolate and pickles.
Bravery thinks about pet respect.

   Ruth Ratcliffe, age 10

From *Painting the Sky: Writing Poetry with Children* published by GoodYearBooks. Copyright ©1995 Shelley Tucker.

Honest Potatoes
Give a Thing a Personality

First, choose an object, a color, or an emotion. Then, answer the
following questions about it. Be sure to write in complete sentences.

      Example: 1. I am a potato.
                     2. I live in the earth and stay warm with a thick, brown blanket.

Start with the words, "I am," shown above, or begin sentences
with the name of the object:

      Example: Potatoes live in the earth with their families.
                Honest potatoes work in underground banks.

1. **What are you?**_____

_____

2. **Where do you live?**_____

_____

3. **What are your favorite colors?**_____

_____

4. **What clothes do you like to wear?**_____

_____

5. **What is your job?**_____

_____

6. **Who are your family and friends?**_____

_____

7. **Where do you go on vacation?**_____

_____

8. **What is your favorite holiday?**_____

_____

9. **How do you move?**_____

NOSE

I am a nose.
I live on a head.
I wear nothing.
My job is to smell
and my hobby is sneezing.
My friends are other noses.
On vacation, I go to Nose York.
I feel nosy.

John Saxon, age 8

MY FRIENDS

I am the ocean,
salty and swirling.
My cousins are the rivers,
the seas, and the lakes.
When I don't have company,
I wave at the sky
because I know
moon or sun will wave back.

Nicholas Quint, age 10

PICKLES

Pickles like to gossip with their friends
In pickle barrels
Rubbing shoulders
Bumping hips
Bobbing in the waves.
They talk excitedly all at once
Happy and safe in their life preservers,
Slurring, glurring, gulping
Giggling, wiggling, jiggling
In their vinegar sea.

Katie Chalfant, adult

Listen to the Sea

Write a poem in which you talk to something in nature. Choose a word from List A or different word that names something in nature. Write it on another sheet of paper.

List A:

sun   stone
moon   night
stars   mountain
sky   dawn
sea   morning

Choose a word from List B or another word that names an action. Write this word next to your word from List A.

List B:

tell   bring
show   look
remind   dance
teach   dream
listen   guide
remember   take

Example:
     Stone, listen.

Then expand your sentence.

Example:
     Stone, listen carefully to the grass as it grows
     around you.

Write more on one subject, or describe other nature words. Then use your favorite lines in a poem.

NATURE

Sun dance me to sleep.
Sea bring me a star.
Sky show me a sunset.
Moon tell me a story.
Star listen to my dream.
Night remember me.
Morning remind me to wake.

Jamie Stroud, age 10

LIGHT

Golden evening light
slowly fading into night's dark cloak,
remember me when you have gone.
Burbling never halting brook,
take me to your mountain home.
Rattling bones, guide me to the land above.

Abraham Koogler, age 9

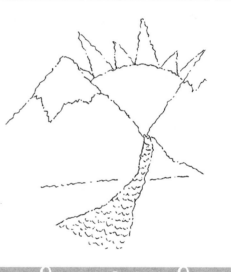

MESSAGES

Night, remind me of yesterday.
Sun, listen to the messages of the clouds.
Moon, look for me on the field.
Sea, guide me to you.
Dawn, bring me to the new day.
Stars, dream me away.
Stone, remember me as a flower in the desert.
Sky, teach me of beauty.
Life, remember my dance.

Kat Gardiner, age 10

Trucks Giggle

Next to the things listed below, write words that name people's actions.

> Example:
>> Trucks giggle.

Then answer: Who? What? Where? When? Why? or How?

> Example:
>> Trucks giggle *(When?)* as they skate on the ice.

On another sheet of paper, use your favorite lines in a poem or write more on one subject.

1. River _____

2. Moon _____

3. Hope _____

4. Love _____

5. Anger _____

6. War _____

7. Staplers _____

8. Sky _____

9. Knees _____

10. Spoons _____

11. Refrigerators _____

12. Memories _____

13. Clock _____

14. Trucks _____

15. Snow _____

16. Tables _____

17. Computers _____

18. Newspapers _____

THE STORM

The ocean roared as the gale winds blew
and the waves danced on the water.
The breeze reached out and took me in its arms
and the storm, it called me daughter.

The rain came pouring down from the heavens
and lightning lit the sky.
Thunder echoed from the mountains
and the wind began to cry.

The trees started to sway like grain
and the fury grew hotter and hotter,
But I was protected from the danger
because the storm, it called me daughter.

Jen Jurdana, age 15

WAREHOUSE ROCK

**Nails dance to country as they swing
their partners around.
Hinges squeak out the blue
because they need oiling.
Shovels clank together
trying to make rock,
but all they get
is heavy metal.**

Elizabeth Browne, age 11

BLOSSOMS

Some blossoms rain
on a shooting star
flying through the dark
black midnight sky,
trying to get to the other world
before their only opening closes.
They have to get through
before daylight wakes.

Erin Britz, age 8

Pianos Wear Tuxedos

On another sheet of paper, write the name of a musical instrument. You may use one of these, or choose a different instrument:

piano	flute
guitar	drums
trombone	tuba
violin	bassoon
bass	clarinet

Pretend the instrument is a person. You might look at the instrument or a picture of it. Then describe it. Name its parts as though it has a human body. Discuss the instrument's legs, teeth, mouth, and ears, and describe the clothes it wears.

Example:

PIANO

Pianos like black tuxedos
and white bow ties.
Their teeth are the color of bones
and they wear braces to keep them straight.
Pianos' shoes are strong, firm,
and made of gold,
so pianos can tap dance
without losing their balance.

FLUTES

Flutes are dressed in copper or gold.
As they pass, you shade your eyes from their glow.
Sometimes they're sweet and soft
but if you push the wrong buttons,
flutes are bitter and harsh
and scream in your ears.
Flutes are skinny
and always ready to sing at a performance.
Flutes are dressed in gold.

Jolene Clampitt, age 12

VIOLIN

Violin,
your hair is like thick spaghetti.
I move my fork
slowly back and forth
in your hair.

Marcy Waldman, age 10

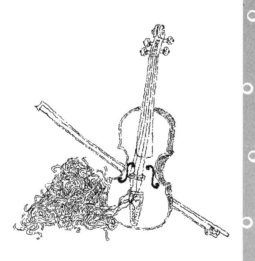

PIANO

Pianissimo *(soft)*
A sweet harmony
Barely heard by human ears
Whispers from the wild
Or daydreams above
Short or long
It sings a soft song
Reminds someone
Of all seasons and holidays.

Fortissimo (loud)
Loud music from a piano
Wild weather
Thunder, lightning
Crashing down
A bear attacking his prey
A dangerous mission
A bunch of yelling people
All in tune.

Jessie Sager, age 12

From *Painting the Sky: Writing Poetry with Children* published by GoodYearBooks. Copyright © 1995 Shelley Tucker.

Stars Speak

Write a poem in which nature talks. First, choose one or some
of the following nature words:

moon	mountain	stone	air
stars	desert	sun	ocean
sky	rainbow	tree	rain
night	earth	forest	shadow
wind	rock	fire	well
breeze	day	cloud	island
tides	valley	coal	granite
flower	weed	galaxy	forest

Then, on another sheet of paper, write a poem in which nature speaks.
You might use some of the following words when you describe
what nature says: talks, asks, whispers, sings, says, tells

Examples:

Islands whisper about bridges.
Coal talks about getting a job as a diamond.

QUESTIONS

Stone asks,
"Why are you so heavy?"
Sun asks, "Why do you change?"
Shadow asks, "Why do you remember?"
Rain asks, "Why do you surrender?"
Breeze asks, "Why do you wander?"
And fire burns all the questions
In one flash.

Laurie Riepe, adult

STARS WHISPER

Stars whisper in the silence of space
while far below
winds sing songs
to sleeping snapdragons.

Caitlin Wright, age 9

SKY AND SUN

A forest sings to the sky.
The day whispers as it goes by.
A flower brags to a weed
and earth beckons to a seed.
The rainbow says goodbye to day
and night comes out to play.

Caroline Tucker, age 11

FIRE

The forest asked the fire,
"Why do you want to harm me?"
The sky said,
"When you burn,
the smoke hurts me too."
A thought,
"Rain, rain,"
clicked into the sky's mind,
and the sky put the fire out.

Juan Castro, age 11

Blue Dreams About Glaciers

Choose a color or texture from the following list or name a different color:

red
green
blue
turquoise
yellow
orange
velvet
silk
satin

Then, on the following lines, answer these questions about it:
1. What are its dreams?
2. What are its thoughts?
3. What does it remember?
4. What does it forget?
5. What does it tell us?

_____

_____

_____

_____

_____

_____

_____

_____

_____

_____

PURPLE

Purple dreams of leading the rainbow.
It thinks of painting velvet.
Purple remembers a long time ago
when it almost forgot beauty.
Purple tells us how to live
and love and learn.

Chloe Melikian, age 11

VELVET

**Velvet likes the night
when she wears coats made of stars.
Velvet thinks about traveling
through the galaxy.
Velvet used to be a rock.
Now she's like a shiny stone
rolled smooth in the ocean.**

Rosie Juarez, adult

SILK

Silk dreams about being warm.
Silk thinks about being red.
Silk remembers to love
and forgets to hate.
Silk tells us to be soft.

Saamanta Serna, age 9

Voice of the Wind

Give a thing a human part, like a voice or heart, and the object
will seem like a person.

Write the names of things, colors, emotions, or ideas on the lines
below. You might name things you can touch or see, like a can opener
or the sky. You might also name ideas, like hope and peace.

Example:

The voice of the rain reminded me to carry an umbrella.

Choose your favorite lines, and, on another sheet of paper, use them
in a poem.

1. The voice of_____

2. The tongue of_____

3. Arms of_____

4. Eyes of_____

5. Heart of_____

6. The mouth of_____

7. Knees of_____

8. The memory of_____

9. The mind of_____

10. The brain of_____

11. The breath of_____

12. The elbows of_____

13. The hearing of_____

14. The feet of_____

15. Ears of_____

16. Hands of_____

17. The shoulders of_____

18. Toes of_____

VOICE OF DAWN

**The voice of dawn
whispered as it crept
through the blackness,
its silvery voice
breaking the shadows.**

Erica Fairchild, age 11

LISTEN

Voice of the river
roars in triumph.
Tongue of the ocean
laps up boats.
Breath of the wind
smells like salt.
Ears of the sea
listen to the animals.

Kellen Rack, age 9

ARMS

Arms of clouds
seem to wrap around the stars.
Night spies on you
as you walk moonless
in the dark.

Hilarie Milligan, age 8

MASHED POTATOES

**Memories of mashed potatoes
are like white thoughts
lumped together.**

Margaret Pearce, age 12

Name _____ Date _____

Tomato Daze

Choose two vegetables or fruits. Write one on each of the top lines.
Then list words to describe the fruits or vegetables.

Example:

watermelon _____

name of vegetable or fruit

green _____

red _____

grape _____

name of vegetable or fruit

raisin _____

peel _____

_____

name of vegetable or fruit

_____

_____

_____

_____

_____

name of vegetable or fruit

_____

_____

_____

_____

On another sheet of paper, write a poem about an ordinary event,
like shopping or doing homework. In this poem, however, use your
fruits or vegetables in the place of people. See if you can include
some of the words you listed on the above lines. Use words like
she, he, her, and *him* instead of *it* to make the fruits and vegetables
seem more like people.

Example:
> Watermelon and grape were best friends.
> In the summer, they played on the beach.
> One day, they sat in the sun too long.
> Watermelon turned a deep red inside
> and grape became a raisin.

STRAWBERRY AND KIWI

Strawberry and kiwi make a great blend.
As they walk down the street
people in cars pull over and watch them pass.

Kiwi's hair is always short and straight
while strawberry's is green and wild.
As different as they are from each other,
together they're a perfect blend.

Jolene Clampitt, age 12

POTATO EYES

Potato had many eyes.
He loved to lay down
and look all around.
Sometimes he played in the dirt
and dug deep holes in the ground.
Potato's friend was pumpkin.
She had beautiful orange skin
and, when she smiled,
she seemed to glow from inside.

Joyce Rifkin, adult

VEGETABLE CLUB

The vegetable club met once a week at the market.
Broccoli, celery, and zucchini
stood up straight in the corner
and talked about prices.
Squash squatted near spinach who wilted from too much heat.
They were proud of their green coats
that kept them warm on cold nights in the refrigerator.

Richard Guevara, age 14

Buses Wheeze

Make a type of transportation seem like a person. On another sheet of paper, write the name of a type of transportation. Choose one of the following or name a different kind of vehicle:

car
truck
airplane
helicopter
van
bicycle
canoe
boat
ferry
ship

Then use human sounds to make that transportation seem like a person:

cough
laugh
cry
sigh
whisper
giggle
sneeze
snore
slurp
talk
wheeze
yell

Example:
My car coughs on the freeway when she is stuck in traffic.

Write more on the same topic, or choose another type of transportation to describe. Then use your favorite lines in a poem.

ON THE SHIP

Waves splash up against the ship,
as the wind whispers to me.
At night stars dance across the sky,
and I can hear them giggle and laugh.

Julie Hall, age 11

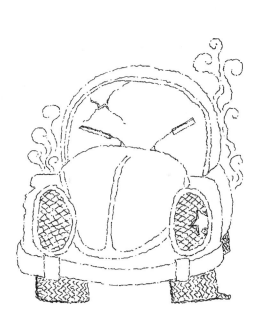

My car sighs
exhausted from the fumes.

My bike moans
too tired to spare a smile.

My van limps
bent out of shape by the heat.

My feet understand
and get ready for a long walk.

Jerome Walker, adult

FERRIES

**Ferries sneeze
when they get water
up their noses.**

Maggie Sudduth, age 9

WHISPER

Cars wheeze from the smell of smoke.
Boats moan when they ache from swimming too much.
Helicopters whisper afraid to be heard.

Crystal Wellman, age 10

From *Painting the Sky: Writing Poetry with Children* published by GoodYearBooks. Copyright ©1995 Shelley Tucker.

Circles Travel in Lines

Choose two shapes or forms from the following lists, or name two different shapes:

line   sphere
arrow   pyramid
triangle   circle
square   octagon
rectangle   hexagon

Then write a poem in which you use one of these ideas:

Tell how one shape or form became the other.
Explain why one wants to be like the other.

Example:

LINES

Three lines were friends
but they had a problem.
They argued a lot and
went in different directions.
The lines decided to put their heads together
and came up with a solution.
Now they form an arrow,
and, when they talk,
find it easy to get to the point.

CUBE

The cube remembers when it was a square,
and lived all day in buildings.
It surveyed the people walking together
and was sad because it was all alone.
One day it found another square.
The squares put four sticks in between them,
and instead of being in a building
they became one.

Morgan Elliot, age 10

THE BIRTH OF THE PARALLELOGRAM

The parallelogram often had dreams
about when he was a square.
He walked down the street
turning head over heels.
One day he tripped on a rock
and that's when his top slid forward.

Sam Garabedian, age 11

THINKING INTO THE THIRD DIMENSION

Circles become spheres
by yawning wide
and wrapping their songs
around each other in big hugs.
Triangles become pyramids
by playing twister with one another,
stretching long legs like spiders
and then kissing the sun.

Laurie Riepe, adult

From *Painting the Sky: Writing Poetry with Children* published by GoodYearBooks. Copyright © 1995 Shelley Tucker.

METAPHOR

A metaphor is the comparison between unlike nouns (persons, places, or things).

Metaphors gain their power from our senses. When a writer names nouns, *(persons, places, and things),* the reader automatically associates the nouns with smells, tastes, touches, sights, and sounds. Because metaphors use one noun to describe another, they create instant pictures. Our senses and experiences show us the meanings of metaphors:

Shoes are hats for the feet.

Karl Hangartner, age 15

Shoes are the brains at the southern end.

Ryan Mackle, age 11

Shoes are solid socks.

Mel Carter, age 18

Writing Metaphors

Metaphors are easy to write. Just compare one noun to another noun with a different meaning. Ask children to complete the sentence, "Love is . . ." Encourage them to name anything they see in the room or out a window, no matter how unlikely it seems at first. Consider the following metaphors: "Love is a glove." "Love is a baseball." "Love is a turnip." These sentences may at first seem unusual. The connections between the nouns within metaphors, however, can always be explained in interesting ways, as in the following example: "Love is a turnip. It is a root of happiness."

The comparison between nouns in a metaphor is usually made with one of these words: *is   are   of*

Is, are, and *of* bridge the nouns in the following metaphors:

A storm is a dance.

Eyes are a story.

Listen to the song of the sky.

How to Use Metaphors in Poems

The following suggestions provide four ways to write poems with metaphors:

1. Choose a metaphor you've written on one of the worksheets, pages 48-67.

> Example:
>> Song of the sky.

Then expand it by answering: Who? What? Where? When? Why? or How?

> Example:
>> The song of the sky *(What?)*
>> hums a melody in the shape of a rainbow.

Next, add more words to your poem:

> Example:
>> The song of the sky
>> hums a melody
>> in the shape of a rainbow.
>> Red, orange, yellow, green,
>> blue, indigo, and violet
>> seem like musical instruments,
>> playing their symphony of color.

2. Select a metaphor you've written on the worksheets, pages 48-67. List words you think of when you read the second, or describing, noun in that metaphor. In the following example, the features of a bicycle, the second noun, describe a song:

From *Painting the Sky: Writing Poetry with Children* published by GoodYearBooks. Copyright ©1995 Shelley Tucker.

A song is a bicycle
                riding
                fast
                coast
                speed
                wind
                carried
                hills
                gears

Use the words from your list or other related words, in any order, to write a poem.

Example:

A song is a bicycle.
When I sing,
I feel like I'm riding
as fast as the wind
carried onto hills
of high notes,
well-oiled
and gathering speed
for the final climb.

You can also compose metaphors in reverse of the typical, metaphorical style. The worksheets on pages 61–67 provide practice writing metaphors with adjacent nouns. These metaphors do not use connecting words like *is, are* and *of.* When the two nouns in a metaphor are adjacent, the first one provides the description. Consider the following metaphor:

banana sea

The noun, sea, is usually described by an article, like *the,* or an adjective, like *huge.* Place an unlike noun in front of it, and it becomes a metaphor.

Nina Munk wrote cucumber mountain and blueberry earth. Her metaphors imply that a mountain is a cucumber and the earth is a blueberry. Nina then listed words she thought of when she read her describing nouns, cucumber and blueberry:

Cucumber mountain

> wet
>
> cold
>
> slimy
>
> crunching
>
> tasty
>
> salt

Blueberry earth

> round
>
> bright
>
> blue
>
> juicy
>
> growing

Next, Nina used some of the words from her list in a poem:

CUCUMBER MOUNTAIN

Cucumber mountain, a rocky journey,
cold, wet, and slimy.
I'm finally there.
One crunch and it's gone.

Blueberry earth,
bright and juicy,
blue and full of life,
the only one I have.

Nina Munk, age 13

When you write metaphors with adjacent nouns, describe the second noun with information about the first.

From *Painting the Sky: Writing Poetry with Children* published by GoodYearBooks. Copyright ©1995 Shelley Tucker.

3. Metaphors often create pictures in a poet's mind. Describe in poetry any pictures you see when you read and write metaphors.

4. Choose a number of metaphors from the one worksheet, and use them in a poem. Metaphors are dynamic even when they begin with the same words. This is because metaphors gather their power from the describing nouns.

I AM

I am a cat playing.
I am blue water, sky, and clouds.
I am a tree, green with a brown trunk.
I am eight years old.
I am the country of sadness and happiness.
I am a window looking to the sky.

Geneva Griswold, age 8

I Am . . .

On another sheet of paper, write the words:

> I am

Then name one of the following:

> an animal
> a color
> an age
> a place
> a feeling
> a food
> a holiday
> an idea
> something in nature

> Example: I am an eagle.

Next make it longer by answering: Who? What? Where? When? Why? or How?

> Example: I am an eagle reminding you of the past.

Continue to write on that subject, or describe another word from the list.

> Example: I am spaghetti tangled on your plate.

Use your favorite lines in a poem.

I Am the Sea

On another sheet of paper, write the name of a thing, place, or event from science, history, geography, nutrition, literature, arithmetic, or computer studies. Begin each sentence with "I am." Complete your sentences with facts about your subject. Choose one of the following topics, or write about a different subject:

the sea	a recipe
an animal	a component of food, like protein
a planet	
	a character in a book
a war	a novel
a treaty	
	a historical figure
a city	
a state	a type of math, like division
a country	
an ocean	a part of a computer

I AM ILLINOIS

I am Illinois, growing in the sunlight and soaking in the rain.
Like the corn of my farmland, I have my family roots.

I am the Midwest, in the middle and somewhere in between
searching for identity between the vastness.

I am the small town, a dot on the map
Where people's lives intertwine to become one.

I am the farmer struggling to exist
Waiting and watching as nature plays its tricks.

I am the tornado twirling and swirling.
I am Illinois all the way through.

        Connie Ingram, adult

BLUE WHALE

I am a blue whale.
I am big and strong.
I almost cover up the whole cave
where the octopus lives.
A blue whale is the size of 30 elephants
and swims in the deep blue sea.

Elliot Smith, age 7

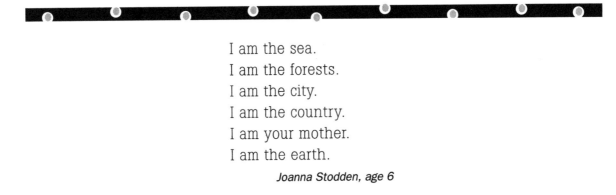

I am the sea.
I am the forests.
I am the city.
I am the country.
I am your mother.
I am the earth.

Joanna Stodden, age 6

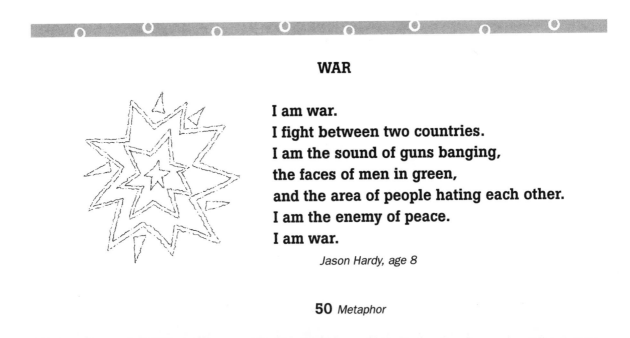

WAR

I am war.
I fight between two countries.
I am the sound of guns banging,
the faces of men in green,
and the area of people hating each other.
I am the enemy of peace.
I am war.

Jason Hardy, age 8

From *Painting the Sky: Writing Poetry with Children* published by GoodYearBooks. Copyright ©1995 Shelley Tucker.

Seasoning

Write the name of a thing next to the words listed below.

> Example: Winter of chocolate

Then answer: Who? What? Where? When? Why? or How?

> Example: Winter of chocolate *(What?)* snowed on my ice cream.

You do not need to do these in order.

1. Dawn of _____

2. Dusk of _____

3. Morning of _____

4. Evening of_____

5. Summer is _____

6. Autumn is _____

7. Winter of _____

8. Spring of_____

9. Twilight of _____

10. Day of _____

11. Night of_____

12. Time of _____

13. Noon is _____

14. Moment of _____

15. Midnight is_____

16. Sunrise of _____

On another sheet of paper, use your favorite lines in a poem, or write more on one subject.

Measure of It

Write the name of a thing next to the words listed below.

Example: Inch of the stars

Then answer: Who? What? Where? When? Why? or How?

Example: Inch of the stars *(What?)* measures the sky at night.

You do not need to do these in order.

1. Inch of _____

2. Ruler of _____

3. Radius of _____

4. A yard is _____

5. Numbers of _____

6. Calculator of _____

7. Amount of _____

8. A foot of _____

9. An angle is _____

10. Arc of _____

11. Measure of _____

12. Count of _____

13. Math is _____

14. Sum of _____

15. Addition is _____

16. Subtraction of _____

On another sheet of paper, use your favorite lines in a poem, or write more on one subject.

From *Painting the Sky: Writing Poetry with Children* published by GoodYearBooks. Copyright ©1995 Shelley Tucker.

From *Painting the Sky: Writing Poetry with Children* published by GoodYearBooks. Copyright © 1995 Shelley Tucker.

Tornado of Applause

Write the name of a thing next to the words listed below.

Example: Hail of telephones

Then answer: Who? What? Where? When? Why? or How?

Example: Hail of telephones *(What?)* rings through the day.

You do not need to do these in order.

1. Tornado of_____

2. A volcano is_____

3. Rain of_____

4. Sleet of_____

5. Sunshine is_____

6. An earthquake is _____

7. Lightning of_____

8. Snow of_____

9. Tidal wave of _____

10. Fog is _____

11. Dew of_____

12. Mist of _____

13. Hail is_____

14. Showers of_____

15. Thunder of _____

16. Avalanches are _____

On another sheet of paper, use your favorite lines in a poem, or write more on one subject.

Price of Peace

Write the name of a thing next to the words listed below.

      Example: Currency of love

Then answer: Who? What? Where? When? Why? or How?

      Example: Currency of love *(How?)* is freely exchanged.

You do not need to do these in order.

1. Cost of_____

2. Money of_____

3. A dime is_____

4. Penny of_____

5. A quarter is_____

6. Dollars of _____

7. Nickel of _____

8. Bank of _____

9. Checkbook of_____

10. A cent is_____

11. Currency of_____

12. Wealth of_____

13. Account of_____

14. Price of _____

15. Value of_____

16. The worth of _____

On another sheet of paper, use your favorite lines in a poem, or write more on one subject.

From *Painting the Sky: Writing Poetry with Children* published by GoodYearBooks. Copyright ©1995 Shelley Tucker.

Roots of Hope

Write the name of a thing next to the words listed below.

> Example: Earth of wonder

Then answer: Who? What? Where? When? Why? or How?

> Example: Earth of wonder *(What?)* keeps me standing.

You do not need to do these in order.

1. Earth of _____

2. Rocks are _____

3. Stone is _____

4. Lava is _____

5. Mountains of _____

6. Valleys are _____

7. Ground of _____

8. Trees are _____

9. Shape of _____

10. Soil is _____

11. Roots of _____

12. Bark is _____

13. Banks of _____

14. Meadows of _____

15. Covering of _____

16. Foundation of _____

On another sheet of paper, use your favorite lines in a poem, or write more on one subject.

From *Painting the Sky: Writing Poetry with Children* published by GoodYearBooks. Copyright ©1995 Shelley Tucker.

RIVER AND SKY

A shallow mountain
with a river running through it—
Zigzagging back and forth,
the river looks like a serpent in the grass.

The sky is crimson,
with true blue.
A cloud comes over.
Someone says it is the shape
of a dragon breathing fire.

Fred Grannam, age 16

EARTH

**The earth is a chessboard,
square and competitive.
Why do people
who live in a round world
take sides?**

**The blue, marbled earth
carpeted with oceans and land
has only one disease,
conflict.**

Ryan Mackle, age 11

From *Painting the Sky: Writing Poetry with Children* published by GoodYearBooks. Copyright ©1995 Shelley Tucker.

White Is Time Ticking

On another sheet of paper, write the name of a color or a texture. Then name things that describe that color or texture.

You may name things you can touch:

> Examples:
> > Black is the ink on the page.
> > Green is the grass blowing in a storm.
> > Velvet is the cat's fur.
> > Cotton is a daisy.
> > Silk is a frozen winter pond.

You may also name things you can't touch:

> Examples:
> > Yellow is hope with the sun in the middle.
> > Red is courage in the morning.
> > White is time ticking.
> > Satin is the fabric of the sky.
> > Wool is a layered cloud.

Then write a poem about one color, or describe many colors and textures
> The title of this exercise was written by Nic Shelton.

RED THINGS

The color red is a tiger, a hot sunny day.
It's a circle and it sounds like a trumpet.
Red is a flame.
It is also angry and strong.
Lava is red and ginger is too.
Ever heard a crazy song? Well, red sings it.
Red is October and a box full of nails.

Nick Grant, age 8

WHAT IS ORANGE?

Orange is the soft fur of a tiger striped kitten,
The warm flames of Christmas fire that put me to sleep
when I'm feeling tired.
Orange is a pair of mittens,
a basketball thrown in the air.
Orange is boiling spaghetti in a great big pot.
It is a pair of boots that have been already bought.
Orange is buttercups, a fish,
a feather from a parrot.
Orange is a carrot that has been picked from a garden.
It is a tiger lily that smells wonderful.
Orange is a tiger that is tame.
Orange is the wildest color you can name.

Lisa Cadman, age 9

Name

Date

I Am Not...

On another sheet of paper, write what you, someone else, or something is not.
Use one or many of the following suggestions.

I am not *(and then name something in nature, like a rock or the moon).*

I am not *(and then name an animal).*

I am not *(and name a color or texture).*

I am not *(and name a place, like a state, city, store, park, etc.).*

I am not *(and name an object, like a stapler, lamp, telephone, etc.).*

I am not *(and name a quality or emotion, like joy, anger, or worry, etc.).*

Examples:
I am not a telephone wire.
A tomato is not a banana.

Make your sentences longer by answering: Who? Where? When? Why?
What? or How?

Examples:
I am not a telephone wire *(Doing what?)* carrying messages.
A tomato is not a banana *(How?)* with a sunburn.

Use your favorite lines in a poem.

A BOY

A boy is not a punching bag
physically or emotionally.

A boy is not a baby
to be given presents
to make you feel better
and then turned away
as you say, "Go to your room.
The adults need to talk in private."
A boy is not a work horse
trying to do everything he can
to please you,
and then being told,
"I'm busy.
I don't have time for a hug."

A boy is just a boy,
trying to be a boy
within the restraints
of an adult world.

Ariel Diaz Stamm, age 12

I am not fog.
I am not a dog.
I am not the color brown.
I am not the state called frown.
I am not a flappy paper.
I am not an angry joy.
I am not a gabby boy.
Let's drop this song of I am not
Because actually, I'm a robot.

Mark Sayre, age 9

I AM NOT

I am not a strawberry all mooshy and red.
I am not a fly squished on a windshield.
I am not yellow blended with the sun.
I am not the Atlantic the home of a whale.
I am not t.v. broadcasting a show.
I am not anger in the wind.

Jaime Nicholl, age 11

Panther Moon

Choose an animal. Write the name of it on the following line:

_____
animal

Example:

kangaroo
_____
animal

On the lines below, describe your animal. You might tell how it looks, what it eats, where it lives, and how it moves.

_____ animal	Example:
	kangaroo _____ animal
_____	tails _____
_____	pouch _____
_____	Australia _____
_____	leap 25 feet _____
_____	clawed feet _____
	eats grass _____

Write the name of your animal on the line below. Next to it, add one of the following nature or time words. Choose a nature or time word that in some way reminds you of your animal and the words you listed about it on page 61.

_____

      animal   *nature / time word*

Nature and Time Words:

days	nights	sky
clouds	mountains	wind
moon	season	autumn
winter	summer	spring
sea	ocean	river
sun	thunder	lightning

Example:
    kangaroo sea

On another sheet of paper, write a poem. Describe your nature or time word using some of the animal words you listed on page 62.

Example:

KANGAROO SEA

When I was eight years old,
I sailed on a kangaroo sea.
It was stormy
and tides whipped through the air like tails.
Sometimes, the waves rose 25 feet
and held in their pouches
driftwood, seaweed, and conch shells,
the treasures of the sea.

GIRAFFE THUNDER

As you walk in a dream, you spot giraffe thunder.
The sound is clumsy and has no definite words.
Its rhythm is eloquent and pulses with lightning.
The sky is a spotted brown canvas with yellow day patches.
On an African savanna, giraffe thunder pounds
and shapes bleached grass into quiet land.
Sound stretches long and catches the lightning.
They merge together into a humped back sky.

Amy Magnano, age 12

SNOW LEOPARD WINTER

Snow leopard winter
creeps along the mountainside.
It is quiet, cold, and gray.
Rocks peek out like black spots.
Snow leopard winter lives alone.

Emily Grosenick, age 7

EAGLE RIVER

Eagle River swoops all day and night.
Eagle River soars like a bird.
Eagle River is elegant and smooth.
Eagle River roars like a carnivore.
Eagle River fishes with me.

Ryan Mattingly, age 10

PANTHER SKY

Panther sky
black and beautiful,
glides like the wind,
and laughs at the clouds.
It jumps over a mountain
in one mighty leap.

Kat Gardiner, age 10

From *Painting the Sky: Writing Poetry with Children* published by GoodYearBooks. Copyright ©1995 Shelley Tucker.

Avocado Sky

Choose a word from the lists below, or select another vegetable or fruit to describe:

cucumber	blueberry	asparagus	apple
banana	avocado	tomato	potato
watermelon	pomegranate	onion	spinach

Write the name of your vegetable or fruit: _____

vegetable or fruit

On the lines below, describe your vegetable or fruit. You might tell how it looks, feels, and smells, where it grows, and any other things about it.

_____

vegetable or fruit

_____

_____

_____

_____

_____

apple

vegetable or fruit

red

juicy

used in pies

star shape inside

peels

has a core

Write the name of your vegetable or fruit on the line below. Next to it, add one of the following nature words. Choose a nature word that in some way reminds you of your vegetable or fruit and the words you listed about it.

_____

vegetable or fruit   *nature word*

Nature words:

moon	mountain	night	breeze	breeze
stars	stream	sun	day	sunset
sky	rain	earth	clouds	fire

Example:

apple   hail
_____

vegetable or fruit   *nature word*

On another sheet of paper, write a poem. Describe your nature word using some of the vegetable or fruit words you listed on page 64.

Example:

APPLE HAIL

Yesterday, the sky turned red and juicy.
Clouds peeled across the sun,
and apple hail fell down,
thick as seeds.
As we ran towards our house,
apple hail opened in our hands
and on the inside
it looked like stars.

WATERMELON STREAM

One day I went to watermelon stream
and saw its colors,
red, green, and white.
All of the little pebbles
reminded me of seeds.
The water looked smooth and juicy.
So take a walk by watermelon stream
and experience its beauty.

Sarah Exum, age 8

POMEGRANATE SUNSET

Pomegranate sunset
seedy, sweet and crisp,
slips beneath horizons
sneaks between the ships.
Red, rosy, round about
riding skies below.
Under, over, all around
becoming melted and yellow.
Pomegranate sunset
mellows and gives a wink.

Amy Roselli Lydum, adult

BIG ROCK CANDY MOUNTAIN

Blueberry streams
and strawberry creams,
lemon moons and banana suns,
near big rock candy mountain,
sweets and treats grow there.

Joanna Tovar, age 8

Cinnamon Rain

Choose a taste word from the lists below, and write it on another piece of paper:

garlic	oregano
pepper	salt
paprika	parsley
chili	cinnamon
lemon	vinegar
sugar	nutmeg
strawberry	vanilla
chocolate	onion

Example:
> Vanilla

Choose a nature word and write it next to your taste word:

wind	mountain
breeze	rain
tide	sky
sky	moon
sun	earth
fire	desert
night	stone

Example:
> Vanilla moon

Describe the taste word.

Example:
> Vanilla moon, white, sweet, flavor, ice cream

Use these and other words in a poem about your nature word.

Example:
> Vanilla moon,
> white in the night sky,
> is round like a large scoop
> of ice cream.

From *Painting the Sky: Writing Poetry with Children* published by GoodYearBooks. Copyright ©1995 Shelley Tucker.

CHOCOLATE MOUNTAIN

One day I visited Chocolate Mountain.
It looked brown with syrup made of ice.
The mountain was a volcano
and when the sun rose in the morning,
it seemed like a chocolate heart.

Melvin Robinson, age 13

GARLIC STORM

Garlic storm signals my nose,
as it beats down in cloves
from clouds that gather
over my head.

James Wu, age 16

CINNAMON RAIN

I see the red brown sky
a rusty, dusty dusk
get washed
by hot steam
we joyfully, cleansingly call
Cinnamon Rain.
It splashes; it plashes
in the dirt.

Dottie Miller, adult

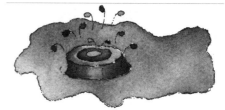

From *Painting the Sky: Writing Poetry with Children* published by GoodYearBooks. Copyright ©1995 Shelley Tucker.

SIMILE

A simile is the comparison between unlike nouns (persons, places, or things) using like or as to make the comparison.

Like a metaphor, a simile compares different things. The simile, however, uses like or as to make the comparison. In the following similes, the words, *like* and *as,* show that tomato is only one of the things that describes hand:

> My hand is like a tomato.
> My hand is red as a tomato.

In a related metaphor, however, the word, *tomato,* completely defines hand:

> My hand is a tomato.

The simile asks the reader to consider a tomato as one possible description of the hand. The metaphor states clearly that the hand and tomato are the same thing. For these reasons, a simile is often easier to understand than a metaphor. A metaphor is generally a bolder statement than a simile. Notice the subtle differences between the following simile and metaphor:

> Simile:
>> My hand is like a tomato,
>> red and peeling from too much sun.

> Metaphor:
>> My hand is a tomato,
>> red and peeling from too much sun.

Basketball Is Like Walking the Sky

Write the name of a sport or hobby on the first line below. Then on the next lines, tell what it is like. You might compare it to an object, like an airplane, or to something in nature, like the moon.

Example:

_____   baseball
_____

sport or hobby   *sport or hobby*

is like   is like

_____   bolt of lightning
_____   hitting the moon
_____   thunder
_____   diamonds
_____   speed of light

Then, on another sheet of paper, use some of the words from your list and other ideas in a poem:

BASEBALL

Baseball is like hitting the moon.
Your bat is as quick
as a bolt of lightning.
The dug-out sounds like thunder
as you seem to travel the bases
at the speed of light.

From *Painting the Sky: Writing Poetry with Children* published by GoodYearBooks. Copyright ©1995 Shelley Tucker.

POEMS ON THE SLOPE

I

Skiing a super, giant slalom course
is like tug of war.
You hang in a tuck.
Your skis chatter
at every turn.
The challenge of holding
onto your angle pulls you
like a magnet down the hill.

II

Ski giant slalom
and the only sound you hear
is snow like waves.

You go down the mountains
like water in streams.
You flow on hills.
Time seems to stop.

It's just you
and the passage of snow.

III

Speed downhill
and you're so self-absorbed
all you can do is race.
You move fast as lightning.

The next gate may be 500 feet ahead,
but it's in front of you
in two seconds.

You don't notice the bitter cold
until the end of your run.
You ache from staying in a tuck
for one minute.

But it's all worth it
for those two seconds between gates
when it feels like you're going
1,000 miles an hour.

Shea Judd-Hume, age 11

Night Falls Like Leaves

Complete one of the following sentences.

       Example: Glaciers glide like skiers.

Then answer: Who? What? Where? When? Why? or How?

       Example: Glaciers glide like skiers *(Where?)* down the sides of mountains.

Continue to write on that subject, or finish other sentences. On another sheet of paper, use your favorite lines and ideas in a poem.

1. Trees move like_____

2. Sun looks like_____

3. Moon seems like_____

4. River is shaped like _____

5. Stars feel like _____

6. Oceans are like _____

7. Rainbows bend like_____

8. Earth is like _____

9. Mountains stand like _____

10. Wind whispers like_____

11. Rain falls like _____

12. Gold appears like_____

13. Glaciers glide like _____

14. Day begins like _____

15. Night ends like_____

From *Painting the Sky: Writing Poetry with Children* published by GoodYearBooks. Copyright © 1995 Shelley Tucker.

SMILE

**A rainbow bends like a smile turned upside down,
not as a frown turned right side up.**

**Just as a rainbow stretches
from one end of the city to the other side,
a smile reaches from one ear to the other.**

Sadie Walker, age 10

NIGHT

Night is the alphabet,
a mass of jumbled lines,
a jag of lightning before thunder,
some needles on some pines.

Night is like a thief,
a game of tic tac toe,
roots from a darkened cave,
an arrow from a bow.

Abraham Koogler, age 9

RAIN

Rain falls like crystals
in magic puddles
on glaciers
standing tall on the earth

Briana Aspini, age 11

From *Painting the Sky: Writing Poetry with Children* published by GoodYearBooks. Copyright © 1995 Shelley Tucker.

Laughter Is as Old as the Sea

Write words on the lines below to finish the sentences. Then, on another sheet of paper, write a poem using your favorite lines and ideas.

Example:
A bicycle is as fast as *a cloud on a windy day.*

1. _____ is as kind as _____

2. _____ is as round as _____

3. _____ is as square as _____

4. _____ is as big as _____

5. _____ is as wide as _____

6. _____ is as flat as _____

7. _____ is as high as _____

8. _____ is as red as _____

9. _____ is as brave as _____

10. _____ is as thick as _____

11. _____ is as caring as _____

12. _____ is as blue as _____

13. _____ is as dark as _____

14. _____ is as white as _____

15. _____ is as wise as _____

From *Painting the Sky: Writing Poetry with Children* published by GoodYearBooks. Copyright ©1995 Shelley Tucker.

SKY, EARTH, AND WATER

**The sky was as mad
as a raging bull,
the earth as hurt
as a rabbit in a snare,
the water as strong as a lion,
but Mother Nature
calmed them all.**

Owen Farcy, age 11

Friendship is as kind as a fawn.
Doubt is as dark as night.
Generosity is as round as the earth.
Love is as brave as an early flower.
Hate is as red as the sun.

Bethany Guldi, age 13

**Soft as ferns
Strong as stones
Tall as forests
Open as valleys
Peace**

Leroy Johnston, adult

LOVE

Love is as wide as the earth.
Friendships are as thick as the sea.
Happiness is as deep as a song,
Laughter in you and me.

Amanda Labrum, age 9

Blue Sounds Like Ice

Choose a word from the following list or select a different color
or texture:

    red
    green
    brown
    black
    turquoise
    lavender
    purple
    orange
    opaque
    transparent
    velvet
    satin
    silk

Then, on another sheet of paper, tell what it:

    looks like
    smells like
    tastes like
    feels like
    sounds like

    Example:
        Green smells like the morning when the grass is mowed.

Write more on that subject, or describe another color or texture.
Then use your favorite lines in a poem.

From *Painting the Sky: Writing Poetry with Children* published by GoodYearBooks. Copyright ©1995 Shelley Tucker.

COLORS

Yellow smells like pollen.
Purple looks like a sunset.
Red tastes like strawberries.
Black smells like smoke.
Orange-red looks like a flare.
Brown feels like tree sap.
Gray smells like clay.
Blue hears like the moon in the sky.
Violet feels like fur.

Yema Evans, age 10

Gray feels cold all over
and tastes like a bitter ice cube.
Gray sounds like silence you hear only in a graveyard.
Gray dreams of a world he has not yet lived to see.

Phoebe Richards, age 12

SUN

**Yellow sun looks like a dime in the sky,
a diamond in space,
and broken crystals.**

Gabrielle Abbott, age 7

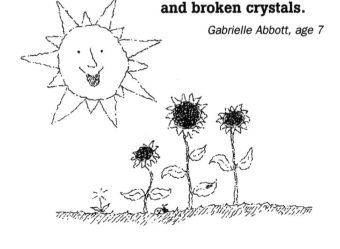

Fast As Popcorn

Complete the following. Then, on another sheet of paper, use your favorite lines in a poem.

1. Happy as _____

2. Mad as _____

3. Disappointed as _____

4. Scared as _____

5. Gentle as _____

6. Kind as _____

7. Surprised as _____

8. Interested as _____

9. Sad as _____

10. Fast as _____

11. Hurt as _____

12. Strong as _____

13. Nice as _____

14. Honest as _____

15. Tall as _____

16. Round as _____

17. Sharp as _____

18. Silent as _____

MOUNTAIN

**A mountain is an ocean
stretching on forever.
Old as a star,
as wise as an owl
covered with trees,
as scarlet as fire,
the moon looks down
on a mountain of gold.**

Sonja R. Carlson, age 11

MAD AS LAVA

Mad as lava
Mad as alligators

as rip tides
as tornadoes
thorns
spiders
traps
Mad as mud.

Dottie Miller, adult

ANIMAL FEELINGS

**Happy as a kitten.
Mad as a tiger.
Disappointed as a snow leopard.
Scared as a cat in a pound.
Kind as a jaguar.
Sad as a panther.
Strong as a mountain lion.
Honest as a bobcat.**

Mary Paquette, age 10

Oceans Move Like Commas

Choose a subject that involves motion. The following are some
possible topics:

> you
> the ocean
> a car
> a bird
> a storm
> a volcano
> an airplane

On another sheet of paper, describe your subject. Compare the way
it looks or moves to the shapes of letters, numbers, and
punctuation marks:

> comma
> period
> semi–colon
> colon
> exclamation point
> question mark
> parenthesis
> quotation marks

> ### WAVES

> Waves start out all splashy and curliqued,
> Gradually bend like fancy S's into plain S's,
> Yield to parentheses,
> And spill flat and smooth,
> Chasing children's feet
> Along the beach
> > *Steve Condit, adult*

THE SKY IS A QUESTION

The sky is a question.
The ocean parentheses
hugging the earth.
The ground is like a cold, hard comma
and the Earth is a period
to end this poem.

Denzil William Leeper Miller, age 11

WATER

Water is like an "S"
sliding off the shore.
A turtle swims in it,
the waves washing off his back.

Kari Miles, age 11

I AM LIKE A SENTENCE

I am like a sentence without a period
and I go on and on,
a bird with a question mark
who soars for an answer,
the ocean with a comma
waiting to be heard.

I am like a car moving along
leaving exclamations behind.
I am a jet, an airplane in parentheses.

Ashley Brown, age 10

WEATHER

A volcano explodes
like an exclamation point
booming, big and bold.
A tornado swirls like a question mark,
twists, turns, and faces upward,
capturing people who wish they knew the answer.

Elizabeth Browne, age 11

IMAGERY

Imagery is a set of mental pictures.

Personification, metaphors, and similes create imagery by working like drawings to show pictures. Poets have additional ways to paint vivid scenes in poetry.

Write detailed descriptions of people, places, and things to create pictures with words. For example, carefully describe a piece of fruit. Write about its size, shape, color, texture, and smell, and the reader will see it easily.

Another way to create images in poetry is through the use of action words. Compare these sentences:

I was excited.

I jumped in the air, shouted with joy, and clapped my hands.

The use of action verbs in the second sentence makes the scene much easier to see.

Use detailed descriptions and action verbs in your poems, and words will be the paint on the canvas of your page.

NIGHT

Mist arises as the blazing sun
sinks into the horizon.
The pale white moon
slides silently
into a quickly darkening sky.
This is night,
and it pulls me
into its peaceful
dream land.

Linnea Mobrand, age 10

Places

We have places for many different things. Some things are kept
in rooms in our houses or apartments. Other things, like jelly and
pickles, are stored in jars. Love lives in our thoughts and hearts.

Write a poem that describes a place. You may fill in the lines
below or use any other ideas you have. To do this exercise,
name a thing, and tell where you store it.

Examples:
> I have a place for motion in my hands and feet.
> She has a place for sunshine in her pocket.

On another sheet of paper, use your ideas in a poem.

I have a place for_____ in_____.

We have a place for_____ in_____.

She has a place for_____ in_____.

He has a place for_____ in_____.

They have a place for_____ in_____.

Our family has a place for_____ in_____.

Our school has a place for _____ in_____.

This city has a place for_____ in_____.

This country has a place for_____ in_____.

Our world has a place for_____ in_____.

Where is your place for_____?

From *Painting the Sky: Writing Poetry with Children* published by GoodYearBooks. Copyright ©1995 Shelley Tucker.

RAINBOWS

**I have a place for rainbows
in my imagination.
I paint them into a dream about ponies
and crystal mountains
with rainbow lights dripping down.**

Brynn Lydum, age 6

A PLACE FOR YOU

A place for you I hold in my heart,
A place for you I keep in my hands,
A place for you I remember in my mind,
That place for you is made of gold.

Lamon Thompson, age 7

PLACE FOR LOVE

I have a place for you in my heart.
We have a place for love in our eyes.
She has a place for hate in the trash can.
He has a place for stars in the sky.
They have a place for friendship between them.
Our world has a place for memory and hope.
Where is your place for peace?

Anna Reisman, adult

Red Slides into First Base

List action words on the following lines:

Example: rolls   Example: crawls

_____   _____

_____   _____

_____   _____

_____   _____

_____   _____

_____   _____

On another sheet of paper, write the name of a color. Next use an action word from your lists to describe the way that color moves:

Example:

Blue jumps in the ocean.

Write more about that color, or choose other colors to describe:

Yellow rushes into the sun.
Blue touches the ocean.
Red swims on a sunset.
Rainbows raise their hands
and colors dive into the sky.

From *Painting the Sky: Writing Poetry with Children* published by GoodYearBooks. Copyright ©1995 Shelley Tucker.

RED WALKS

Red walks on the moon.
Yellow touches the sky.
and then black makes it gloomy.
Orange fights fires.
White swims in blue water.
Purple jumps up and down
watching peach compete
in the Olympics.

John Mayer, age 10

ACTION

White crashes into the snow.
Blue flies toward the sky.
Yellow jumps into the sun.
Green lunges into buses and
Purple runs into blue and red.

Blake Matthews, age 9

A TOUCH OF COLOR

Purple splashes a plum
and red covers a ball.
Black fills the night sky
while yellow paints a banana.
The world spins around
so all the colors can fly.

Tiffany West, age 12

Action

List words that name actions.

Example: sing   Example: roll

_____   _____

_____   _____

_____   _____

_____   _____

_____   _____

_____   _____

On another sheet of paper, write a poem. Start some or all of your lines with
an action word.

WEAVE MY DREAMS

Weave my dreams.
Sew the questions.
Crochet a web to hold my thoughts.
Stitch the comfort of a friend.
Knit the silence like a ghost.
Shape the night into a blanket.
Paint your feelings and hold them close.

Angela Lewis, age 17

From *Painting the Sky: Writing Poetry with Children* published by GoodYearBooks. Copyright ©1995 Shelley Tucker.

Mind Tennis

On the first line below, write the name of something you like to do or a place you like to go. Some examples are playing the piano, riding a bike, and going to the movies. On the next lines, write action words *(verbs)* that describe it.

_____

something you like to do or place you like to go

_____

_____

_____

_____

Example:

use the computer
_____

something you like to do or place you like to go

turn it on
_____

wait
_____

watch
_____

work
_____

save
_____

Then, on another sheet of paper, use some of the words from your list and other ideas in a poem:

COMPUTER

Turn it on.
Look up and down.
Write and rest.
Save and wait.
A computer
is tennis for the mind.

NATURE

Whisper with the wind at night.
Talk to the sun like a friend.
Shine like the stars when you're sad,
and burn like a fire when you're angry.
Be full of power and learn from nature.
Then you can
sing like the birds,
show your strength,
roll like the waves,
and be calm.

Julie Hall, age 11

PRANCING FROGS

Dancing fairies and prancing frogs
Hop and bounce over logs.
Flying high are butterflies.
Playing pixies sing and dance.
We're in fantasy land.
Writing pencils
Let our minds soar.

Tiffany Dierking, age 12

AUTUMN

Enjoy the leaves
as they descend down your throat.
Sip the colors slowly
so you can appreciate the beauty
and taste the last days of light.

Erin Schlumpf, age 11

REPETITION

Repetition in a poem is the use of the same words or lines two or more times.

When a writer composes an essay about drumming, he or she probably repeats the word, *drum,* to link together the paragraphs.

In poetry, writers also repeat words and lines to make transitions. Repetition in poetry serves other functions, too:

The sound of a poem contributes to its meaning: The repeated word: drum

    drum

    drum

creates the sound of drumming.

Repetition in poetry acts like the foundation, beams, and roof of a house to give a poem its shape:

DRUM

Listen to the sound
drum
drum
drum
beating a tempo
for thunder,
for rain,
for hot days.
Sun drums down
on your head,
keeping rhythms
of the seasons.

Repeated words and phrases allow the writer to emphasize
an idea:

> I wake up ready
> each morning.
> I greet the new day
> each morning.
> I give thanks for you
> each morning.

Repetition in a poem may seem like lyrics in a song:

THE RAIN

The rain is a dancer
waiting to dance.
The rain is a singer
waiting to sing.
Rain, I am waiting for you.
Come down
Come
down to me.

Sarah Exum, age 8

Writers repeat different parts of speech in poems.
Repetition of a noun helps define it. Repeated prepositions
emphasize temporal or spatial relationships. Repetition of verbs
and adverbs places additional focus on the action in the poem.

The following are lists of subordinating conjunctions,
words that join two clauses of unequal value:

Subordinating Conjunctions

after	though	although	unless
as	until	because	when
before	whenever	if	where
since	while		

From *Painting the Sky: Writing Poetry with Children* published by GoodYearBooks. Copyright © 1995 Shelley Tucker.

Consider the following clause, "unless we get the money." It starts with a subordinating conjunction and raises the question, "Then what will happen?" Begin lines of poetry with subordinating conjunctions, and suggest a series of questions:

UNLESS

Unless we stop war,
unless we practice peace,
unless we recognize
the value in differences,
unless we see the similarities
between all people,
then our symphony of voices
will play out of tune.

Juanita Frye, adult

Behind Night Is Day

Fill in some of the following lines. You do not need to do these in order. Then, on another sheet of paper, use your ideas in a poem.

Example:

> Inside peace and hope,
> inside memories and beliefs,
> inside this moment,
> there is quietness that balances
> outside.

Inside_____

Inside_____

Inside_____

Above_____

Above_____

Above_____

Across_____

Across_____

Across_____

After_____

After_____

After_____

Before_____

Before_____

Before_____

Beyond_____

Beyond_____

Beyond_____

During_____

During_____

During_____

Near_____

Near_____

Near_____

Outside_____

Outside_____

Outside_____

Over_____

Over_____

Over_____

Toward_____

Toward_____

Toward_____

Through_____

Through_____

Through_____

Under_____

Under_____

Under_____

From *Painting the Sky: Writing Poetry with Children* published by GoodYearBooks. Copyright © 1995 Shelley Tucker.

THE EVERGREEN MEADOW

Beyond all your thoughts, wishes, and hopes,
Vacations of hot weather and ski slopes,
Beyond all fantasies and dreams,
And beyond all the flavors of ice cream,

There's an evergreen meadow.
The evergreen meadow always stays green,
Stays green through the cold snow of winter,
And the rainy storms of spring.

Through the hot weather of summer,
And the misty atmosphere in fall,
The evergreen meadow stays green.

Lisa Cadman, age 9

TOGETHER

Unite together
for we are the weather.
The moon, the stars,
they're what we are.
All of Mother Nature's kinds,
all of Father Time's designs,
all the life and all the joy,
every single girl and boy.
From elephant to tiny ant,
from sketch to sing to skip and dance,
from love and anger, laughter, impatience,
this is the glow of earth's creation.

Maya Miller, age 14

TOWARD

Toward the moon
Toward the stars
Toward a dream
Toward a challenge
Toward an accomplishment
Toward a goal
Toward is hope.

Suzanne Howard, adult

Inside

On another sheet of paper, write a phrase from List A:

List A
In my mother's
in my father's
In my brother's
In my sister's
In our
In my school's
In my

Then add a word from List B:

List B

eyes	memory
heart	love
hands	fear
house	sadness
mind	joy
shoes	family
smile	

Example:
     In our hands

Use this phrase to start your poem.

    Example: In our hands are interconnecting highways and flowing rivers.

Now write a poem. Repeat your opening phrase, and add other ideas to it.

    Example:
        In our hands are interconnecting roads and flowing rivers.
        In our hands are skies with unlimited views.
        In our hands are the rain forests and the cities.
        In our hands are choices about our land.

From *Painting the Sky: Writing Poetry with Children* published by GoodYearBooks. Copyright © 1995 Shelley Tucker.

I SEE LOVE

In my mother's wishes,
In my father's dreams,
In my little brother's hands,
And in my sister's needs,
I see love.
I see love.

Where waves may sometimes hit the rocks,
Where things at times are bound in locks,
We are still together
And I see love.

Kathryn Schosboek, age 10

IN MY SISTER'S EYES

In my sister's eyes, I see memories.
In my sister's eyes, I see my family.
In my sister's eyes, I see my sister
who will never stop being my friend.

Heather Linker, age 10

OUR MINDS

In our minds
we see future peace.
In our minds
we see people working together.
In our minds
we see green forests.
In our minds
we think of how nice it will be
when there's no more hate
in our world.

Faye Satta, age 11

I Have a Dream

On another sheet of paper, write the words:

I have a

Then add one or more of the following:

prayer   promise
hope   message
request   blessing
story   heart

Use your ideas in a poem. Start some of your lines with the words, "I have."

DREAM

I have a dream someday the heavens
will come down and touch the earth,
and for many years and as far as the eye can see,
peace will fill the land.

I have a dream that men, women and children
all over the world will shake hands across the seas
and war will not be in their vocabularies.
Alison Katica, age 9

From *Painting the Sky: Writing Poetry with Children* published by GoodYearBooks. Copyright © 1995 Shelley Tucker.

SEASONS

I have a dream that comes only in winter.
My dream in winter is ice and coldness in the air
and piles of snow on the streets.

I have a dream that comes only in spring.
My dream in spring is flowers coming out
and the scent of roses filling the air with happiness.

I have a dream that comes only in summer.
My dream in summer is kids playing in pools,
splashing cold water on roads,
and walking on hot sand at the beach.

I have a dream that comes only in autumn.
My dream in autumn is leaves falling
in the morning from brown branches,
raking them in a big pile, and jumping in.
I have a dream
of the seasons of the year.

Lisa Cadman, age 9

DREAM

I have a dream that the sea
will be as blue as the sky
and grass as green as my eyes.
Coldness will turn into warmth.
Stars will touch the earth.
I have a dream that clouds will open up
and let me into their world.

Kathleen Keibel, age 10

INQUIRY

An inquiry is a question.

When someone asks a question, the response is often factual. In poetry, answers are realistic and imaginative. The exercises in this chapter ask questions that are like diving boards. The writer jumps off. Where will he or she land? In poetry, air, clouds, and sky are reasonable substitutes for water.

WHAT DID YOU DO TODAY?

I went to Vashon Island
and we made footsteps in the sand.
They were bigger than a cat's
which are the same size as a snake's
except a snake doesn't have feet.

Caitlin Wilson, age 4

WHERE'S THE SUN?

The sun's up high.
Never eat the sun
because the sun is made of fire.

Caitlin Wilson, age 4

Invention

Think of something you would like to do or have done for you. No machine, however, exists that can do it. This is your chance to invent that machine.

On the lines below, answer these questions about it. Please write in complete sentences.

  What is your machine called?
  What does it do?
  What does it look like?
  What other machines do you think of when you look at it?
  What does it move like?
  What does it sound like?

Then on another sheet of paper, use your ideas in a poem.

_____

_____

_____

_____

_____

_____

_____

_____

_____

_____

_____

_____

_____

From *Painting the Sky: Writing Poetry with Children* published by GoodYearBooks. Copyright © 1995 Shelley Tucker.

MOPPER POPPER

It washes and mops
and does flip-flops.
It's long and skinny
and looks like a popsicle.
Mopper Popper moves
with a shimmer and a glide.
It sounds like a lion
with a drum inside.

Lauren Hubbard, age 9

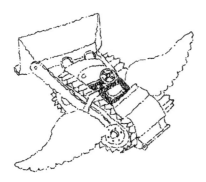

BULLFLY

My machine is called Bullfly
and it pushes the clouds.
It's yellow and big.
Bullfly sounds like an airplane
and moves really fast.
Bullfly is a bulldozer with wings.

Michael Clark, age 8

A JELLY BEAN MACHINE

A jelly bean machine
invented in a dream,
it doesn't do its name
but only makes ice cream.
It wiggles when it talks
and talks while squirting blocks
of sherbet – orange, green, and pink
and rocky road and peppermint
and almond fudge, I think.
And flower flavored malteds,
and chocolate flavored shakes,
and ice cream cones so cold,
they make my stomach ache.

A jelly bean machine
shaped like a tiny train,
great big nose, lantern eye,
but long legs like a crane.
And since it can go up and down
and in and out the doors,
we've had to put a freezer
on every single floor!

Steve Condit, adult

From *Painting the Sky: Writing Poetry with Children* published by GoodYearBooks. Copyright © 1995 Shelley Tucker.

What's in the Ocean?

On another sheet of paper, name something, and say what's in it. Choose one of the following, or name a different subject:

What's in . . . ?

> rain forest
> volcano
> ocean
> desert
> solar system
> hope
> joy
> sadness
> tears
> Japanese house
> French store
> the library
> the human body

You may name things that are really in it:

> What's in the ocean?
> Starfish and oysters,
> waves turning surfers
> upside down.

You may also name things that are not really in it:

> What's in the ocean?
> The hope of sailors,
> songs of fish
> and stories of seashells
> waiting to be told.

From *Painting the Sky: Writing Poetry with Children* published by GoodYearBooks. Copyright © 1995 Shelley Tucker.

What Does this Key Unlock?

On another sheet of paper, write one of the following questions:

What's behind this door?
What does this key unlock?
What do I see out this window?
Where does this path go?

Then answer your question. You may give factual answers.

Example:
    What does this key unlock?
    This key unlocks doors and drawers,
    cabinets and safes.

You may also give imaginary answers, or use both fact and fantasy:

Example:
    What does this key unlock?
    This key unlocks numbers
    stacked up and down,
    added in checkbooks
    counted on cash registers.

    Numbers work in banks
    and count calories
    in cakes and cookies
    I love to eat.

A GARDEN

Where does this door lead?

This door leads to a garden
where the sun sets
and the moon rises
in your hand.

Alison Katica, age 9

WHAT'S IN THE SKY?

I see clouds soaring, purple and pink.
I see sun and rain, yellow and blue.
I see my rainbow of colors,
violet, indigo, blue, green,
yellow, orange, and red.
I see my rainbow,
drifting away the clouds.

Rebecca Moorman, age 7

KEY

This key unlocks white
which takes the shape of sheep,
colors the mountains,
rolls down the river,
and rests at my door.

This key unlocks a blue gem
which lights up and takes
the shape of the sky,
colors the flowers with dew
and becomes part of rivers.

Nari Baker, age 10

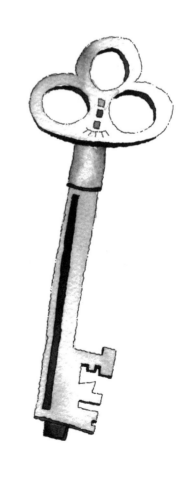

What If Time Forgot?

On another sheet of paper, write:

What if time

Then add one or more or the following:

forgot?
repeated?
expanded?
disappeared?
danced?
joked?
destroyed all clocks?
only remembered holidays?
stood still?
moved backwards?
turned inward?
collapsed?
told us what it wanted?
gave us its secret?
moved at different speeds?
talked?
remembered?

Answer your question in a poem.

WHAT IF TIME DANCED?

What if time danced?
Would it prance around
in and out of different dimensions
and float through the sky like a cloud?

What if time danced?
Would it remember old secrets,
and would it whisper them to us?

Natasha Williams, age 11

WHY?

Why aren't the stars in the sky
moved by the wind?
Why does the earth turn
but never go anywhere?
Why do we get older
instead of younger?
What if time knows these answers?

Julie Rosenbaum, age 9

TIME

What if time collapsed?
Mountains would crumble to the ground.
The moon would fall from the sky.
Oceans would be soaked up by the earth.

What if time stood still?
You would feel
like you were in a picture.

What if light were destroyed?
It would always be dark.
You would be frozen in fright
and wonder,

Where has light gone?
When will it come back?

And you would know,
that only time can tell.

Stephen Harvey, age 10

What's Inside the Alphabet?

Choose one of the letters in the alphabet. On another sheet of paper, write
what is inside that letter. You may name words that start with the letter:

Example:
>Inside the letter *w*
>are walruses, whales, and wrens,
>washing machines, water sprinklers,
>and wishing stars
>whistling their favorite songs.

You may also name things or animals that remind you of the shape of the letter:

Example:
>Inside the letter *w* are two *v's*
>trying to find their way home.
>
>Inside the letter *w* is a child.
>She is standing on the ground
>and reaching with both hands
>towards the sky.

Then use your ideas in a poem.

INSIDE C

Inside the letter C
are some cats in cradles
and cranky kangaroos.
They all sing a silly song, called,
"Cockadoodle doo."
Now they're going to sleep,
cuddling and cozy.
Goodnight.

Claire Carlson, age 8

INSIDE THE LETTER T

Inside the letter *t*,
I am twirling on the tip
of a top, writing tongue twisters,
and playing with my turtle.

Kristina Russell, age 9

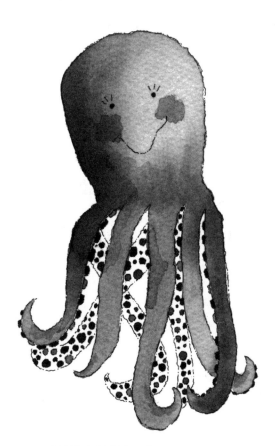

THE LETTER O

Inside the letter o are
opossums, otters, octopuses,
orcas, and oxen.

Opossums like the outside.
The outside likes the otters.
Otters like octopuses.
Octopuses like orcas.
Orcas like oxen.

Ashley Denherder, age 9

From *Painting the Sky: Writing Poetry with Children* published by GoodYearBooks. Copyright © 1995 Shelley Tucker.

From *Painting the Sky: Writing Poetry with Children* published by GoodYearBooks. Copyright © 1995 Shelley Tucker.

What If We Exchanged Up for Down?

On another sheet of paper, write: What if. Then add one word or phrase from lists A, B, and C, below, to form a question.

List A:
I
we
they
you
she
he

List B:
substituted
exchanged

List C *(Use these or different pairs of words):*
white for black
up for down
inside for outside
yesterday for tomorrow
night for day
chocolate for vanilla
bikes for cars
ocean for sky
circles for lines
summer for winter
chocolate for spinach
peace for war

Example:
> What if they substituted peace for war?

Then answer the question.

Example:
> What if they substituted peace for war?
> Then helmets would be used as flower pots.

Write more on this subject, or ask new questions and answer them.

UP FOR DOWN

What if we exchanged up for down?
Would people fall out of the sky?
With rain falling up
and plants growing down,
and clouds for oceans,
we'd fall up to the ground.

Gabrielle Abbott, age 7

EXCHANGE

What if I exchanged
up for down
silly for stern
circles for lines
smile for frown
cool for burn
prose for rhymes?

What if I exchanged
hands for feet
socks for pants
shirt for shoes?

Then you'd
read about me
in the news.

Rudie Singer, adult

WHAT IF WE EXCHANGED SAFETY FOR VIOLENCE?

What if the world today were peaceful?
What if people knew the difference between right and wrong?
What if children were able to play on all street corners without having to worry?
What if the violence just disappeared and things were no longer problems?
What if all people could be caring and loving to one another?
What if what if was a reality?

Brooke Weiner, age 11

ALLITERATION

Alliteration is the repetition of the same consonant sound at the beginnings of words.

Alliteration is like rhyme. When poems rhyme, the same or similar sounds occur at the ends of words. Alliteration, on the other hand, repeats the same consonant sounds at the beginnings of words.

Alliteration allows a poet to create the silk of snow, the blast of a bullet, the whisper of wind, and the molding of mud through sounds used at the beginnings of words in a poem.

MASTERLY MUG

With the manipulation of masterfully molded mud
I manufactured my mother's mug.
Then I glazed it to a glittering green
And when it came back I wanted to scream.
My masterly molded mug had been
Mugged by another's mug.

Craig Terry, age 9

Jelly Jams in Jars

Choose one of the following letters:

    b, c, d, f, g, h, j, k, l, m, n, p, q, r, s, t, v, w, x, y, z.

Write the letter on a line below. Then write words that start with the sound of the letter. These may be unrelated words or words that form sentences.

    Examples:

        scissors, sang, celery, Sandy, sit

        Tall Tom ate every tasty tomato.

On another sheet of paper, use some of your words, sentences, and ideas in a poem.

Sweet red strawberry
you sound
like an opera singer
swinging in the wind.

Adrian Arnold, age 9

JUNGLE

Near nightfall,
misty, tumbled jungle comes alive.
Lanky vines move
in slow deliberate slithers.

Mel Carter, age 17

QUAPPAPLE

My name is Quapple,
But I changed it to Quappaple,
Then Quadrapple,
Then Quadraplemaple,
Then Quarople,
Then Quotation,
Do you have a question?

Mari Anderson, age 10

WINTER WORDS

A sound whispers softly in my ear as snow falls.
It is not the summer sun
nor is it the wind.
It says, "As I make a drop of snow
and as I wonder,
I think of the first snow.
I know I loved it."
It is the sound of winter words.

Kathryn Shosboek, age 10

Bashful Bananas

On the lines below, write the name of a fruit, vegetable, or animal that starts with the same sound as the word listed on the line.

> Examples: *b.* Bashful bananas always prefer to travel in bunches.
> *p.* Polite pelicans wait their turn in line to fish.

You do not need to do all of these. On another sheet of paper, use your favorite lines and ideas in a poem.

b. Bashful_____

c. Confused_____

d. Dressy_____

f. Friendly_____

g. Green_____

h. Honest_____

j. Jealous_____

k. Kind_____

l. Lazy_____

m. Merry_____

n. Nighttime_____

p. Polite_____

q. Quiet_____

r. Red_____

s. Slimy_____

t. Two_____

v. Victorious_____

w. Worried_____

y. Youthful_____

z. Zany_____

Dancing Donuts

On the lines below, write the name of a fruit, vegetable, or other thing that starts with the same sound as the word listed on the line.

Examples: *d.* Dancing donuts always try new steps.
k. Kissing kites get caught in clouds tossed by the wind.

You do not need to do all of these. On another sheet of paper, use your favorite ideas and lines in a poem.

b. Bragging _____

c. Caring _____

d. Dancing _____

f. Flying _____

g. Greeting _____

h. Hiking _____

j. Joking _____

k. Kissing _____

l. Laughing _____

m. Missing _____

n. Naming _____

p. Painting _____

q. Quilting _____

r. Reading _____

s. Skating _____

t. Talking _____

v. Visiting _____

w. Whistling _____

y. Yelling _____

z. Zipping _____

From *Painting the Sky: Writing Poetry with Children* published by GoodYearBooks. Copyright © 1995 Shelley Tucker.

CARING CARROTS

Caring carrots ask the limp lettuce,
"Are you okay?"
Greeting grapefruits say
"Good morning" to muffins.
Hiking hyacinths sing in unison
as they march along.
Laughing lilies' sense of humor is contagious.

Nancy Waldman, adult

Confused cats count counter clockwise.

Cassie Abel, age 9

Polite pelicans pick pansies.
Quiet quails quiver.
Red roosters remind ravens.
Slimy slugs slurp spaghetti.
Two turtles take time turning.

Genny Ansden, age 9

Caring cats clown around.
Dancing dogs dodge donuts.
Flying fish do flip-flops.
While greeting gophers gobble down gumdrops.

Courtney Irby, age 10

ONOMATOPOEIA

Onomatopoeia is the use of words that suggest or sound like the sounds, objects, or actions they name.

Slurp, bang, splash, meow, hiss, **and** *slide* **are examples of onomatopoeia.**

Words are symbols that stand for things, ideas, people, feelings, actions, and descriptions. Onomatopoeia not only names a sound, an object, or a movement, but evokes it, too.

The use of many onomatopoeic words in a poem generally gives it a humorous tone, and places the stress on sound or motion. A poem with one, two, or three onomatopoeic words, allows the suggestion of sound and action to work more subtly, and integrate with the visual aspects of the poem.

Please refer to the lists of onomatopoeic words on page 120. Vary the number of these words you use in your poems, and then notice how onomatopoeia affects both sound and meaning in poetry.

CAT

This cat does not just meow.
It squeaks and rustles
and I really wonder how
it manages to splash, crunch
and make a whole bunch
of ding donging and squeaking.
When all the bird can do is yackety yak.
This cat is definitely no ordinary cat.

Sarah Moorman, age 10

Yikes!

On another sheet of paper, write the name of a place or an animal that has a lot of sounds.

   Example:
      dog

Make a list of these sounds:

   Example:
      yikes
      growled
      bow wow
      slurped
      smooched
      soothed
      woof

Then use some of the words from your list in a poem. You may also use the following sound and action words.

Sound and Action Words:

bang	lunge	slap	crash
beep	meow	slurp	creak
blink	moan	smack	crunch
boom	moo	snap	cuckoo
bow wow	munch	splash	ding dong
buzz	murmur	squeak	drip
chirp	ping pong	squeal	fizz
clang	quack	squish	flip-flop
clap	rattle	swirl	grate
ring	click	thump	gurgle
rip	clink	ticktock	hiss
roar	cluck	whisper	honk
rustle	crack	yackety yak	
sizzle	crackle		

From *Painting the Sky: Writing Poetry with Children* published by GoodYearBooks. Copyright © 1995 Shelley Tucker.

Yikes!
dog lips
kissed me
on the nose,
slurped the dirt
between my toes,
smooched and nibbled
at my ear, licked away
a salty tear,
soothed and scraped
a wounded knee......
dog lips
seem to follow me!

Ann Teplick, adult

In the night,
hiss,
munch,
eat,
purr,
screech,
pounce,
cat.

Danielle Stewart, age 9

ICE CREAM SHOP

**Fizz, fizz is the noise
in the ice cream shop
of root beer splashing into vanilla.
Crack is the sound of the crystal clear clink
of the cherries bouncing on the sides of a glass.
Slurp, slush are the noises of the boy
who swirls on the stool.
Beep, honk are the sounds of New York
outside the ice cream shop.**

Jana Krinsky, age 10

Purple Roars

On another sheet of paper, write the name of a color.

>   Example:
>   Red

Then add one or more of the following sound words to it.

babbles	meows
bleats	oinks
chuckles	quacks
giggles	roars
groans	screeches
gurgles	squeaks
hiccups	squeals
hisses	whispers
honks	whistles
hums	yelps

>   Example:
>   Red whispers.

Next, answer: Who? What? Where? When? Why? or How?

>   Example:
>   Red whispers at the dark.

Write more on the same subject, or describe other colors. Use your favorite lines in a poem.

FRIENDS

Red whispers at the dark
telling it to stay away.
Blue giggles in the sea
as it sways forever.
Purple laughs quietly
knowing it is blue and red.

Alex deSteiguer, age 11

POETRY EXERCISES THAT GIVE ADDITIONAL SUPPORT

Some children benefit from additional support when they first write poetry.

The models in this chapter are like bicycles with training wheels. They take children on journeys with excellent views, and insure they'll successfully arrive at their destinations.

BROWN

Brown,
When it's young and growing,
And deep and rich
Feels rough like bark on a tree trunk or
Crumbly compost living by the garden.
And when it's old and worn and faded
Brown feels soft like fine powdery dirt
Filtering between your fingers
Or smooth like hard, bare ground.
Brown.

Ellie Davis, adult

Blue Is the Season of the Sky

Choose a color. Write it at the beginning of each line.
Then complete the sentences.

_____ reminds me of _____

_____ tastes like _____

_____ has the sound of _____

_____ is a box of _____

_____ is the season of _____

Love Knows About Friends

Choose a feeling. Write it at the beginning of each line.
Then complete the sentences.

_____ is the color of _____

_____ wishes for _____

_____ knows about _____

_____ moves like _____

_____ wears _____

_____ shows us about _____

_____ has a pocket of _____

From *Painting the Sky: Writing Poetry with Children* published by GoodYearBooks. Copyright © 1995 Shelley Tucker.

Winter Wears White

Name a time, season, or month. Some choices are:

morning, afternoon, evening, night, dawn, dusk, summer, autumn, winter, spring, January, February, March, April, May, June, July, August, September, October, November, December

Write your time, season, or month at the beginning of each line.
Then complete the sentences.

_____ is the color of_____

_____ reminds me of_____

_____ wears_____

_____ lives_____

_____ friends are_____

_____ remembers_____

Rain Dreams About Clouds

Choose something in nature like a tree, the sun, the moon, the sky.
Write it at the beginning of each line.
Then complete the sentences.

_____ dreams about_____

_____ remembers_____

_____ moves like_____

_____ is the promise of_____

_____ vacations_____

_____ is a sign of_____

From *Painting the Sky: Writing Poetry with Children* published by GoodYearBooks. Copyright © 1995 Shelley Tucker.

Hope Has a Pocketful of Peace

Choose an emotion or quality listed below, or name a different feeling:

love
hate
sadness
happiness
joy
courage
guilt
anger
envy
laughter
hope
secrets
strength
friendship
gossip
honesty
marriage
divorce
peace
war

Then, on another sheet of paper, use some or many of the following to describe it. You do not need to do these in order:

is a box of
is the song of
is the of month of
is the year of
tastes like
is shaped like
is a memory of
dreams of

remembers
is the touch of
is a dance of
is a season of
looks like
feels like
has a pocket of
sounds like

BLUE

Blue is a whale.
It is rainy weather on a windy night.
Blue is shaped like a robin's egg just about to hatch.
Blue sounds like the ocean.
and feels soft like cotton.
Blue makes me feel happy on a gloomy day.
It is a lake on a bright sunny morning.
Blue tastes like a glass of water.
Blue is the song sadness.
Blue is the month of February.
and a box of velvet.

Cary Davis, age 10

PEACE

Peace is a box of songs and the sound of flowers.
Peace is the shape of a tree and the height of a mountain.
Peace dances the breeze that cools the hot day.
Peace reminds you of the value of friendship and safety.
Peace has no pockets.
It shows you everything it has
and then peace gives it all to you.

Wymon Harmon, adult

LAUGHTER

Laughter is a box of peanuts
and the song of purple.
Laughter is shaped like an oval
and dreams about feelings.

Laughter is a dance of friends
and the season of spring.
Laughter sounds like a bird
and carries a pocket of seasons.

Maiya Exum, age 9

From *Painting the Sky: Writing Poetry with Children* published by GoodYearBooks. Copyright © 1995 Shelley Tucker.

SYMBOL

A symbol is a word, picture, movement, or sound that stands for something else.

A symbol is similar to metaphor because both equate one thing with another. Consider the following metaphor: Love is the sun.

If *love* = a and *sun* = b, then one way to represent a metaphor is: a = b.

Like a metaphor, a symbol also equals something else. The symbol, however, is usually more difficult to use in poetry because it only states one part of the equation: a or b.

The sun, for example, may stand for love in a symbolic poem about it. A poet uses the properties of the sun, rays, light, and warmth, to suggest love, without naming the word:

> Sun rays surround me.
> I grow in its light
> and feel the warmth
> of sun in my heart.

Because only one half of the equation is stated in the main body of a symbolic poem, people often have different ideas about what the symbol represents. In the poem shown above, for example, the symbol, sun, might mean love, family, summer, or air. Because of the range of ideas about the meaning of a symbol, the symbol at first seems to have broader application than a metaphor. The reverse, however, is true. The inherent qualities of a symbol limit what it can represent. The sun, for example, is bright, hot, and light. Because of its characteristics, it is unlikely that a poet would use the sun to represent dishonesty, shadows, or night.

In a metaphor, on the other hand, any two things may be equated. Then the explanation about the meaning of the metaphor rests with the poet who forges the connection, as in the following metaphor: The sun is dishonesty in disguise.

Read symbolic poems with children, and ask them what the symbols mean. This exercise demonstrates the differences in interpretation of a poem. It also shows that symbols might be accurately interpreted in a variety of ways.

Some symbols are assigned their meanings. A stop sign on a street corner and a certificate awarded to a child, for example, have no inherent meaning. The most powerful symbols in poetry, therefore, draw on nature. A star, the clouds, and a forest naturally transfer their inherent characteristics to the things they symbolize.

STAR

A star lost among the clouds
shines in silence.
A fireball roars
larger than ten million suns,
rolls through the light years,
lost in the woods,
a memory.

A spark in the black
points to a promise,
a great dipper
of cosmic space,
where dreams are born
in the ink that runs.

But for the point of light,
the eye, the book
would be empty.

Victor James Helleberg, adult

Name _____ Date _____

Eyes

A symbol stands for something else. Choose a type of a color, part of the body, feature of a house, or thing in nature that might serve as a symbol. The following are some possibilities:

red	hand	door	flower
black	eyes	window	wind
white	teeth	key	shadow
green	face	room	night
blue	heart	chair	snow
yellow	lungs	walls	tree

Write your symbol on the first line. Then, on the next lines, list what it stands for or represents.

Example:

_____ *blue* _____   _____
symbol   *symbol*

_____ ocean _____   _____

_____ sky _____   _____

_____ lakes _____   _____

_____ lines on paper _____ _____

_____ sad _____   _____

_____ jeans _____   _____

_____ ink _____   _____

Use the words you listed and write a symbolic poem in one of the following ways.

1. Write some or all of the words from your list. At end of your poem write:
   What am I?

   Example:
   Ink
   lakes
   ocean
   sky

   What am I?

2. Choose some of the words from your list, and then write more about them.
   Use your symbol as the title or as the last word:

   Example:
   Oceans reflect the sky,
   lines of ink roll on paper like lakes
   calm enough for canoes,
   another name for sorrow,
   blue.

3. Use some or all of the words from your list. After each, write an action word.
   Include the following words in your title or last line: What am I?

   Example:
   What Color Am I?
   Oceans dive.
   Skies reach.
   Lakes rest.
   Sad sings.
   Jeans travel.
   Ink blots.

From *Painting the Sky: Writing Poetry with Children* published by GoodYearBooks. Copyright © 1995 Shelley Tucker.

SUN and MOON

Sun
A yellow, gold circle
brings life towards the earth
and a new day forward.
It keeps things growing,
sings its nature song over the world.
covers the earth with colors,
then sets, and it is night.

Moon
A white circle with different shapes,
puts everything to sleep
as it works its way around the earth.
It brings up nocturnal animals to hunt their prey,
dances like a white, round gown
waiting until morning comes.
Then it disappears behinds the clouds
and it is morning.

Jessie Sager, age 12

RAINBOW

A multi-colored half circle in the sky,
a joyous scene everybody loves,
comes out to promise after a rainfall
that the earth will never be flooded.

Jessie Sager, age 12

Gold

A symbol stands for something else. The sun, for example, is a star, and it is also a symbol. The sun represents life, warmth, and hope.

Choose something in nature that serves as a symbol. Pick a word from the following lists, or choose a different symbol:

moon	mountain	sun	gold	star
tree	fire	ocean	Earth	rainbow

Write your symbol on the first line, and then list what it represents:

Example:

water
symbol   *symbol*

life

change

motion

power

calm

drink

From *Painting the Sky: Writing Poetry with Children* published by GoodYearBooks. Copyright © 1995 Shelley Tucker.

Choose a word from your list to describe in a poem, and circle that word
or underline that word.

Example:

_____
water

symbol

_____   _____
life   calm

_____   _____
change   drink

_____   _____
motion   strength

_____
<u>p</u>ower

Now, write a poem about the circled word, but do not include that word in
your poem. Instead, use your symbol and some of the other words from your
list to describe the word you circled or underlined. In the following poem, the word
described is *power*.

Example:

WATER

Water is a force
like a bull raging,
a volcano erupting,
and an avalanche writing a message
down the side of a mountain.

Water changes a landscape.
Rivers carve new paths
through the earth.

Other times water is calm
and seems to rest.
But never underestimate water.
It gathers strength
while it sleeps.

SEA

Sea come to me.
Your beauty and grace
remain a mystery.
Sea your waters so blue,
sailboats come to your waters.
Sea come to me.
I will always hold you.
Your oceans are mine.

Sarah Exum, age 8

LIGHT

**Flashing by I see the light
running to get to safety
skipping stairs two at a time.
Dashing, flipping, flopping,
I see the light
running from the night.**

Elizabeth Browne, age 11

AFTER THE STORM

Everything is peaceful.
Stars shine like gold.
The sun's story is told.
Lightning is calmed,
and the moon
guards the sky
all night
unharmed.

Jessie Sager, age 12

From *Painting the Sky: Writing Poetry with Children* published by GoodYearBooks. Copyright © 1995 Shelley Tucker.

PARADOX AND SYNESTHESIA

Paradox and synesthesia are often difficult to contemplate and challenging to write because at first they appear to make no sense.

Paradox

A paradox is a statement that seems to contradict itself but contains a truth. Consider the following paradoxical statement:

Failure is opportunity.

Initially, this sentence seems to contradict reason, but the truth in a paradox emerges with closer inspection. When someone fails, that person also learns what doesn't work. A failure might represent new opportunities for future success.

SKY BALL

The moon plays ball with the sun.
Catching the reflection,
the moon throws it back
in one fast pitch,
a home run for the night sky.

Monte Justin, adult

The model, Day Understands Night, on page 139, provides practice in writing paradoxes.

Synesthesia

Synesthesia is the description of one sensory perception by another. Synesthesia is often challenging to write because it contradicts the experience of the body. The following sentence is an example of synesthesia:

Smell the rainbow.

A rainbow has no smell, but an explanation can be made: Smell the grass, green, like the color of a rainbow. Synesthesia, however, leaves out the explanation, and asks the poet and reader, instead, to sense the connection.

SIP THE MOON

It's made of milk
and soothes your stomach.
So if you're ever feeling down,
taste the world.
Just be sure
to leave some for me.

Phoebe Richards, age 12

The models, The Color of Courage, page 141, and Touch the Moon, page 143, provide practice in writing synesthesia. Taste the beauty in poetry when one sense describes another.

From *Painting the Sky: Writing Poetry with Children* published by GoodYearBooks. Copyright © 1995 Shelley Tucker.

Day Understands Night

1. On another sheet of paper, write a pair of opposite words from **List A:**

dark	light	sun	moon	wealth	poverty
day	night	up	down	truth	lies
front	back	white	black	failure	success

2. Then select one of the following words from **List B:**

> knows
> remembers
> tells about
> understands

> Example:
>> *(From List A:)* dark   light
>> *(From List B:)* understands

3. **Now write a sentence in which you put the word or words from List B** *between* **the words from List A**

> Example:
>> Dark understands light.

4. **Next expand your sentence or thoughts by answering: Who? What? Where? When ? Why? or How?**

> Example:
>> Dark understands light. It is home of the moon and stars.

5. **Then add new ideas to your poem.**

> Example:
>> Dark understands light.
>> It is the home of the moon and stars.
>> Dark wears sunglasses the color of the sky
>> and like a curtain lifts at dawn.

From *Painting the Sky: Writing Poetry with Children* published by GoodYearBooks. Copyright © 1995 Shelley Tucker.

WHITE UNDERSTANDS BLACK

Wealth remembers poverty
Like gold and brass
One follows the other in silence.

Color follows darkness
Like the sunset into the night
They know each other
As friends on a beach.

White understands black
Like the sun and the moon
The moon reflects the sun with joy
But the sun does not look back.

Matthew Berley, age 10

TRUTH AND LIES

Truth knows lies.
Truth knows what it could have said
but didn't.
If truth did not understand lies,
it could not be truth.

Lies also know truth
and lies hate it
because truth fights its way to the top.

Lies struggle to become the truth.

Dashel Schueler, age 11

WEALTH KNOWS POVERTY

Wealth knows poverty
but pretends not to see it.
Truth knows lies
but pretends not to hear it.
Right understands wrong
but pretends not to feel it.
Failure remembers success
and is bitter about not living it.
We all know things
we wish we could not remember.
We all know things
we don't want to taste, see, or hear.

Jolene Clampitt, age 12

From *Painting the Sky: Writing Poetry with Children* published by GoodYearBooks. Copyright © 1995 Shelley Tucker.

The Color of Courage

On the lines at the bottom of this page, write:

What is the color of

Then add a word from the following list, or name another human emotion, quality, or condition:

courage

hope

peace

laughter

war

happiness

rage

joy

sleep

memories

respect

anger

Example: What is the color of sleep?

Next, answer your question. Write on one subject, or describe different emotions.

_____

_____

_____

_____

_____

_____

_____

_____

_____

_____

_____

COLOR OF MEMORIES

What are the colors of memories?
Green like gently rolling hills?
Blue like the sky of spring?
Orange like a thousand smiling jack-o-lanterns?
Or blank, the color of amnesia?

Kat Gardiner, age 10

THE COLOR OF PEACE

The color of courage is red and loud,
and it stands out bright and proud.
The color of peace is white like geese
with graceful wings.
It looks at you and sings.

Gina Griffith, age 13

DREAMS

Purple is the color of dreams.
When ready for night,
it teaches you something new,
taking you somewhere
you've never been before.
Sometimes purple gets excited
and your dreams become chaos.
But usually purple stays calm
and wakes you with a smile on your face.

Phoebe Richards, age 12

From *Painting the Sky: Writing Poetry with Children* published by GoodYearBooks. Copyright © 1995 Shelley Tucker.

Touch the Moon

On another sheet of paper, write one of these words:

      taste   touch

Then add a word or words from the following lists to it.

a rainbow	hope
the moon	courage
the sky	sadness
the sun	anger
a cloud	happiness
	joy
a dream	love
a memory	hate

Example:
    Touch the sky.

Write more on your first subject, and add new ideas to your poem:

Example:

    Touch the sky.
    Sometimes it's blue
    and moves like the ocean
    with clouds for waves.

    Touch the sky.
    At night it's dark
    like a cave
    with faint stars,
    bears hibernating
    for the winter.

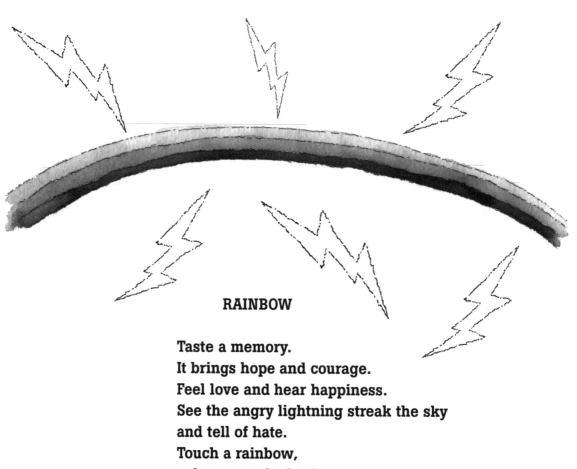

RAINBOW

Taste a memory.
It brings hope and courage.
Feel love and hear happiness.
See the angry lightning streak the sky
and tell of hate.
Touch a rainbow,
a dream on the horizon.

Sonja R. Carlson, age 11

TOUCH A MEMORY

Touch a memory.
It's slippery and hard to catch.
Touch a dream.
It can be soft or rough.
Taste hate.
It's never any good
and sometimes,
it makes you sick
to your stomach.

Molly Hancock, age 11

TASTE THE SKY

Taste a cloud, the sky, the sun,
hate, and anger.
Touch a dream a memory
love, happiness, and joy.
Taste and touch as much as you can,
for life is sweet
or bitter if you wish.

Jolene Clampitt, age 12

GENERAL GLOSSARY

From *Painting the Sky: Writing Poetry with Children* published by GoodYearBooks. Copyright © 1995 Shelley Tucker.

Alliteration	the same beginning consonant sound in two or more words close together
Edit	alter to make more suitable; prepare for publication
Free verse	poetry without end rhyme, set structures, or meter
Haiku	a traditional Japanese form of poetry consisting of three lines with 5-7-5 syllables per line
Imagery	a mental picture
Inquiry	a question
Limerick	a traditional humorous form consisting of five lines; lines one, two, and five are long and rhyme. Lines three and four are short and rhyme
Metaphor	the comparison between two unrelated nouns
Meter	regular patterns of heavily and lightly stressed syllables
Mood	the tone of a poem reflecting the author's attitudes, feelings, and perspective
Onomatopoeia	the formation of words that sound like or suggest the objects or actions being named
Paradox	a statement that seems to contradict itself but contains a truth
Personification	the assignment of human traits to things, colors, and ideas
Poem	a compact piece of writing with intentional line breaks that contains one or more poetic elements, the fundamentals and foundation of poetry, e.g. metaphor, simile, personification, imagery, alliteration

Rhyme	repetition of similar or identical sounds
Simile	a comparison between two unrelated nouns using "like" or "as" to bridge the connection
Sonnet	traditional structure written in meter consisting of fourteen lines of three quatrains and a couplet
Stanza	a group of lines forming a structural division of a poem similar in appearance to a paragraph
Symbol	a sign, sound, word, or object representing a thing, a quality, or an idea
Synesthesia	the description of one sensory perception by another

From *Painting the Sky: Writing Poetry with Children* published by GoodYearBooks. Copyright © 1995 Shelley Tucker.

YOUNG CHILDREN'S GLOSSARY

Alliteration	the same sound at the beginning of different words
Edit	change
Imagery	a picture in your mind
Metaphor	comparison between two different things
Onomatopoeia	words that sound like sounds
Personification	making things seem like people
Repetition	write again
Simile	comparison between two different things using "like" or "as"
Symbol	one thing stands for another
Synesthesia	one sense describes another

BIBLIOGRAPHY

Poetry books for use with children and teenagers

Adoff, Arnold; Pickney, Jerry. *In for Winter, Out for Spring*. Harcourt Brace Jovanovich, 1991.

Bly, Robert. editor. *News of the Universe, Poems of Twofold Consciousness*. Sierra Club Books, 1980.

Dunning, Stephen; Lueders, Edward; and Smith, Hugh. editors. *Reflections on a Gift of Watermelon Pickle*. Scott, Foresman, 1966.

Dunning, Stephen; Lueders, Edward; and Smith, Hugh. editors. *Some Haystacks Don't Even Have Any Needle*, Lothrop, Lee, 1968.

Fleischman, Paul. *Joyful Noise: Poems for Two Voices*. Harper Trophy, 1988.

Hughes, Langston. *Selected Poems*. Vintage Books, 1974.

Kennedy, X. J.; Kennedy, Dorothy. *Talking Like the Rain*. editors. Little, Brown, 1992.

Koch, Kenneth; Farrell, Kate, editors. *Talking to the Sun*. The Metropolitan Museum of Art, 1985.

Schenk de Regniers, Beatrice; Moore, Eva; White, Mary; Carr, Jan. editors. *Sing a Song of Popcorn*. Scholastic, 1988.

Schwartz, Alvin. *A Twister of Twists, A Tangler of Tongues*. J. B. Lippincott, 1972.

Stafford, William. *Stories That Could Be True*. Harper and Row, 1977.

Sullivan, Charles. editor. *Imaginary Gardens*. Times Mirror, 1989.

Worth, Natalie. *all the small poems*. Farrar, Straus and Giroux, 1987.